7th CENTURY EGYPT

SITES IDENTIFIED IN THIS TEXT
Ancient names in parenthesis.

D1544937

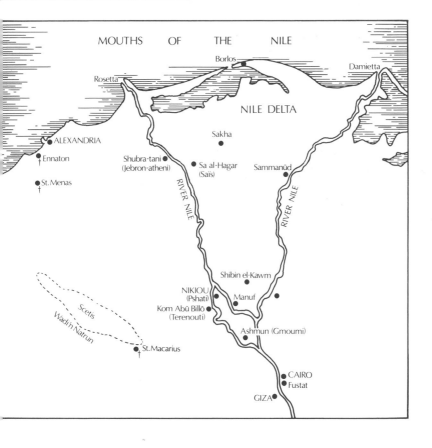

MOUTHS OF THE NILE

Borlos

Rosetta

Damietta

NILE DELTA

ALEXANDRIA

Ennaton

St. Menas

Shubra-tani
(Jebron-atheni)

Sakha

Sa al-Hagar
(Saïs)

Sammanūd

RIVER NILE

RIVER NILE

Shibin el-Kawm

NIKIOU
(Pshati)

Kom Abū Billō
(Terenouti)

Manuf

Ashmun (Gmoumi)

Scetis

Wādi'n Natrun

St. Macarius

CAIRO
Fustat

GIZA

CISTERCIAN STUDIES SERIES: NUMBER ONE HUNDRED AND SEVEN

MENA OF NIKIOU

‡

THE LIFE OF ISAAC OF ALEXANDRIA

THE MARTYRDOM OF SAINT MACROBIUS

CISTERCIAN STUDIES SERIES: NUMBER ONE HUNDRED AND SEVEN

MENA of NIKIOU

The Life of
ISAAC of ALEXANDRIA
&
The Martyrdom of
SAINT MACROBIUS

Introduced, Translated, and Annotated
by
David N. Bell

Cistercian Publications
Kalamazoo
1988

A translation of *Phbios mpiniŝti mpipatriarchēs ethouab ouoh piarchēepiskopos nte tiniŝti mpolis Rakoti abba Isaak,* edited by E. Porcher, *Patrologia Orientalis 9/3* (Paris, 1915).

The work of Cistercian Publications is made possible in part by support from Western Michigan University to the Institute of Cistercian Studies.

Available in Britain and Europe from
A. R. Mowbray & Co Ltd
St Thomas House   Becket Street
Oxford OX1 1SJ

Available elsewhere (including Canada) from the publishers
Cistercian Publications
WMU Station
Kalamazoo, Michigan 49008

Library of Congress Cataloguing in Publication Data:

Mēna, of Nikiou.
  [Life of Isaac of Alexandria]
  The life of Isaac of Alexandria ; and, The martyrdom of Saint Macrobius / Mēna of Nikiou ; translated, with an introduction by David N. Bell.
    p. cm.
  Bibliography: p. 135
  Includes indexes.
  ISBN 0-87907-407-8. ISBN 0-87907-607-0 (pbk.)
  1. Isaac, of Alexandria, d. 692. 2. Macrobius, Saint.
3. Christian martyrs—Egypt—Biography—Early works to 1800.
4. Persecution—Egypt—History—Early works to 1800. I. Bell, David N., 1943-   . II. Mēna, of Nikiou. Martyrdom of Saint Macrobius. 1988. III. Title. IV. Title: Life of Isaac of Alexandria. V. Title: Martyrdom of Saint Macrobius.
BR1608.5.I83M46   1988
270.2'092'4—dc 19
[B]   88-4298
                                                          CIP

Typeset by Gale Akins, Kalamazoo, Michigan
Printed in the United States of America

LIST OF ABBREVIATIONS

ACE   A. J. Butler, ed. (with a most important Additional Bibliography) by P. M. Fraser, *The Arab Conquest of Egypt* (Oxford
       1978² [originally published 1902]). Fraser's edition also contains Butler's *The Treaty of Miṣr in Ṭabarī* (originally published at Oxford in 1902), and his *Babylon of Egypt: A Study
       in the History of Old Cairo* (originally published at Oxford in
       1914). Butler's work remains indispensable.
CSCO   *Corpus Scriptorum Christianorum Orientalium*
GCAL   G. Graf, *Geschichte der christlichen arabischen Literatur,
       Studi e Testi* 118ff (Vatican City, 1944–1953).
HP   Severus/Sāwīrūs ibn al-Muqaffaʿ, ed./tr. B. Evetts, *History of
       the Patriarchs of the Coptic Church of Alexandria,* PO I: 99
       [1]-214 [116]; PO I: 379 [115]-518 [254]; PO V: 1 [255]-
       215 [469]; PO X: 356 [470]-551 [665] (rpt. Paris, 1947-48).
       The pages of the four parts are numbered consecutively in
       brackets from (1) to (665), and it is this pagination which is
       followed here.
ODCC   F. L. Cross, ed., *The Oxford Dictionary of the Christian
       Church* (Oxford, 1958).
PO   *Patrologia Orientalis.*
SAJ   *Le Synaxaire Arabe Jacobite (Rédaction Copte),* ed./tr. R.
       Basset, PO I: 215 [1]-380 [166]; PO III: 243 [167]-546
       [470]; PO XI: 505 [471]-860 [826]; PO XVI: 185 [827]-
       424 [1066]; PO XVII: 525 [1067]-782 [1324]; PO XX: 742
       [1325]-790 [1374] [Tables] (Paris, 1907-1929). As in *HP*
       above, the pages of the six parts are numbered consecutively
       in brackets from (1) to (1374), and it is that pagination which
       is followed here.
SE   De Lacy O'Leary, *The Saints of Egypt* (New York, 1937; rpt.
       Amsterdam, 1974).

Amélineau, *Géographie*
    E. Amélineau, *La géographie de l'Égypte à l'époque copte* (Paris,
    1893; rpt. Osnabrück, 1973).
Amélineau, *Histoire*
    E. Amélineau, *Histoire du patriarche copte Isaac,* Publications de

v

l'École des Lettres d'Alger: Bulletin de correspondance Africaine II, (Paris, 1890). In Coptic and French.

Crum, *Dictionary*
W. E. Crum, *A Coptic Dictionary* (Oxford, 1939; rpt. 1979).

Hyvernat, *Actes*
H. Hyvernat, *Les Actes des martyrs de l'Égypte* (Paris, 1886; rpt. Hildesheim, 1977).·

Lampe, *Lexicon*
G. W. H. Lampe, *A Patristic Greek Lexicon* (Oxford, 1961; rpt. 1978).

The Life of Shenoute
Besa, *The Life of Shenoute,* trans. D. N. Bell, CS 73 (Kalamazoo, 1983).

Mason, *Greek Terms*
H. J. Mason, *Greek Terms For Roman Institutions: A Lexicon and an Analysis,* American Studies in Papyrology 13 (Toronto, 1974).

Porcher, *Vie*
E. Porcher, *Vie d'Isaac, Patriarche d'Alexandrie de 686 à 689, Patrologia Orientalis* 9/3 (Paris, 1914; rpt. Turnhout, 1974). In Coptic and French.

A NOTE ON NOTES

There are four sets of Notes in this volume:

A) notes to the Introduction to the *Life of Isaac of Alexandria;*
B) notes to the translation of the *Life;*
C) notes to the Introduction to the *Martyrdom of Saint Macrobius;*
D) notes to the translation of the *Martyrdom.*

They are cited simply as A, B, C, and D, with the appropriate note number. E.g. See A, n. 4 = See note 4 to the Introduction of the *Life of Isaac;* Cf. D, n. 16 = Compare note 16 to the translation of the *Martyrdom of Macrobius.*

Finally, the following four abbreviations are used for languages: Bo = Bohairic Coptic; Sa = Sahidic Coptic; Gr = Greek; and Lat = Latin.

Psalms are cited according to the Hebrew enumeration.

CONTENTS

INTRODUCTION

THE HISTORICAL AND
THEOLOGICAL BACKGROUND

IN THE MIDDLE OF THE FIFTH CENTURY Constantinople and much of the christian east was in a state of theological ferment. The monolithic church of the early fathers had been split into a considerable number of quarrelling sects and factions, each convinced of its own infallibility, and each equally convinced that all the others were guilty of the foulest heresy and inevitably doomed to eternal torment. There were supporters of Nestorius, supporters of John of Antioch, supporters of Eutyches, supporters of Leo, and supporters of a whole variety of views and opinions which were neither quite one thing nor quite the other. The Nestorian controversy had been born in misunderstanding and misrepresentation, and by the middle of the century there was little doubt in most people's minds that the patriarch of Constantinople was guilty of teaching that Mary had given birth to a mere man. That this was quite untrue was also quite irrelevant: then, as now, it was not what a person said which was significant, but what others believed him to have said. And the eminently successful propaganda of Cyril of Alexandria had convinced the majority of those who listened that Nestorius had denied the divinity of Christ and asserted that Jesus was not God.[1] This is not to say that Nestorius was guiltless. He was not the spotless lamb of Constantinople sacrificed on the eager altar of Alexandria. Not only was he intemperate in his language (foolhardy might be a better word), but his explanation of the way in which the godhead and the manhood were conjoined in the one person of Jesus of Nazareth was indeed open to suspicion. A union *kat'eudokian*[2] is a loose-ish sort of union, for the Greek word *eudokia* means good pleasure, or will, or wish, or favour, and if God is conjoined with man in Jesus by no more than divine favour there is little to distinguish Christ from a super-prophet or a maxi-saint. Cyril, then, was quite right to be suspicious of Nestorius's ideas and terminology, but quite wrong to put it about that he denied Christ's divinity. This Nestorius never did (and Cyril knew it), but despite his protestations of innocence—he was still protesting in the rambling *Bazaar of Heracleides* written in exile in his last years[3]—the Cyrilline version of Nestorianism became the accepted and established version.

Cyril's watchword, borrowed as he thought from Athanasius the Great (but in reality—and ironically—derived from the heretical Apollinaris of Laodicea) was 'one nature of the divine Word enfleshed'.[4] But by 'one nature (*physis*)' Cyril meant one person, one individual human being, and he was not implying that the divinity and humanity had become mixed up or confused. Indeed, he says, anyone who maintains this is simply gabbling.[5] Nevertheless, there was a real ambiguity about the term *physis*. It could be interpreted to mean either 'nature' or 'person', and it is obvious that such ambiguity could lead to unfortunate misunderstanding. To acknowledge Christ in two natures is very different from confessing him to be two people; and to say that Jesus of

Nazareth was one person is very different from maintaining that in him the godhead and manhood could no longer be distinguished.

Alexandria and Egypt stood firmly behind Cyril, as they had always stood firmly behind their patriarchs, and Cyril's terminology—'one nature of the divine Word enfleshed'— became accepted egyptian terminology. Cyril's triumph over Nestorius at the Council of Ephesus in 431 was therefore celebrated with jubilation and glee, and the banishment of Nestorius first to his monastery in Antioch and then to the remote south of Egypt was considered to be proper and just. Shenoute the Great, who had attended Cyril at Ephesus, considered that Nestorius was accursed and that he deserved to have his tongue cut out, and the voice of Shenoute is here the voice of egyptian monasticism in general.[6]

The *Formulary of Reunion* signed in 433 between Cyril and John of Antioch, Nestorius's foremost supporter, established an uneasy peace which lasted some twelve years. It was a peace founded on unwilling compromises and concessions, and was doomed to failure from the start. It could be sustained only for as long as Cyril and John were there to sustain it; John died in 441 and Cyril in 444. Cyril's successor was Dioscorus, a man who was ultra-Cyrilline in his sympathies, and Dioscorus allied himself with the Court Chamberlain, the eunuch Chrysaphius, and the muddled archimandrite Eutyches to form a dangerous triumvirate which plotted to overthrow the precarious peace of 433, to crush 'Nestorianism' (as they understood it) once and for all, and to re-establish ultra-Cyrilline orthodoxy as the official creed of the empire. How they went about this and precisely what they achieved need not here concern us, but as we observed at the beginning of this introduction, by the middle of the fifth century their ill-judged efforts had divided the christian world into a collection of violently antagonistic sects and factions, and something had to be done about the situation with all possible haste.

The new emperor Marcian, aided, abetted, and guided by his formidable wife Pulcheria, therefore called a council–the great Council of Chalcedon, the fourth ecumenical council–which was attended by more than five hundred bishops and which convened in the church of St Euphemia the Martyr on 8 October 451. Leo the Great, the forceful and intelligent Roman Pontiff at the time, had also been invited to attend, but he replied that precedent and his own responsibilities prevented him from doing so. Nevertheless, he said, he would certainly be present with the bishops in spirit and would send papal legates to represent his person and act as the voice of the see of Peter. In any case, Leo had already prepared–or, with the assistance of his secretaries, had had prepared–a formal doctrinal statement of his own position. This document, the so-called *Tome of Leo,* strongly condemned both Nestorius and Eutyches, and although the council for which it had originally been drafted–the Ephesian council of 449 which was wholly controlled by Dioscorus–had totally rejected it, the circumstances at Chalcedon were radically different. Leo's *Tome* was there received with shouts of approval: it was acknowledged as representing the faith of the Fathers; it was seen to stand in the tradition of the Apostles; its teachings (said the bishops) were the teachings of Cyril, and cursed by anyone who dared teach otherwise.[7]

At the Council of Chalcedon Nestorius, once again, was condemned; Eutyches and Dioscorus were deposed and exiled (the third member of the triad, Chrysaphius, had already paid the supreme penalty; without any trial he had been executed before the gates of Constantinople on the orders of Pulcheria); both Cyril and Leo were acclaimed as the voices of orthodoxy; and the holy fathers at the council drew up an official summary statement of their views on the relationship of the divine and the human in the one person of the incarnate Christ. But this summary statement, for all its good intentions, led to disastrous results, for it stated categorically that Christ was 'made known in *two* natures (*physeis*) without confusion, without change, without division, and without separation'.[8]

By 'nature' (*physis*), the fathers of Chalcedon meant 'nature'; they did not mean 'person'. They taught, unquestionably, that in Christ there was an unconfused union of godhead and manhood in which the divinity and humanity were distinct but not separate; united but not mixed together. In other words, what they had tried to express was what contemporary Christianity actually accepts; it was the way in which they expressed it that led to dissension, violence, and murder.

Leo, the West, and the Byzantines accepted the 'two natures' formula from the start. Alexandria and Egypt immediately rejected it. For them, in the heritage of Cyril, 'two natures' meant 'two persons', and they had no intention of dividing the one Christ and resurrecting, in all its infamy, the hideous heresy of Nestorius. Christ was not 'God-in-man', nor yet 'God-with-man'; he was 'the God-man'! *Two* natures after the Incarnation? Never! What had Cyril said? '*One* nature of the divine Word enfleshed.' And if Cyril had said it, it was true. The Egyptians therefore rejected the Council of Chalcedon, rejected the dyophysite, or 'two-nature-ite' doctrine, and thus established what came to be known as the Monophysite Church. These were to be followed in due course by the Ethiopians, the Syrian Jacobites, and the Armenians, and they have remained a church separated from the rest of the orthodox world ever since.[9]

It is difficult to exaggerate the ill-feeling, antagonism, and just plain hatred that this schism produced. Dioscorus's unfortunate successor, Proterius, a chalcedonian appointment with chalcedonian beliefs, was beaten to death in Alexandria and his body burned in the local hippodrome. Dioscorus himself—a deposed and exiled heretic as far as the Chalcedonians were concerned—was lauded as a saint and a martyr by the Monophysites.[10] Severus (Sawīrus) ibn al-Muqaffa', the monophysite bishop of El-Ashmūnein in the later tenth century, speaks of Dioscorus as enduring persecution for the orthodox faith and of preserving it in the face of great adversity, 'until he received the crown of martyrdom on the island of Gangra'.[11] The reason for his trials, Severus adds, was the subservience of the Council of Chalcedon to the will of its imperial masters—Marcian and Pulcheria—and, as a consequence, 'the members of that council and all the followers of their corrupt creed are called Melkites, because they follow the opinion of the prince and his wife, in proclaiming and renewing the doctrine of Nestorius'.[12] The term 'Melkite' (*malakīya* in Severus's Arabic) derives from the Syriac word *malkāyā,* 'imperial', and, in all probability, was first applied to the Chalcedonians by the Monophysites only some years after Chalcedon (the earliest instance I know of its use dates from about 460). It was a derogatory term—'emperor's men' implies 'imperial lackeys'—and was never used by the Chalcedonians to describe themselves.

The monophysite successor of the deposed and sainted Dioscorus was Timothy Aelurus, who again, says Severus, suffered from hardships and from continual battles with the Chalcedonians.[13] He was also exiled to Gangra, and although he was recalled to Alexandria in 475, his position there was extremely unstable. The emperor Zeno (whom we shall meet again in a moment) virtually had pen in hand to banish him again when death anticipated him, and Timothy died, condemned by the Melkites and commended by the Monophysites, in the year 477.[14] By 475, however, the Monophysites controlled not only Alexandria and Egypt but also Antioch, and taking advantage of the absence of its chalcedonian bishop Martyrius (he was away from his see looking for allies in his struggle with the very people who were about to supplant him), they installed in his place Peter the Fuller. He, too, suffered for the faith: he was imprisoned, deposed, and imprisoned again, but he regained his position in 482 and remained patriarch of Antioch until his death in 488.[15]

It was by this time obvious to everyone, including the

emperor Zeno, that Monophysitism had very strong popular backing. It was spreading rapidly in Syria and Palestine as well as in Egypt, and even Acacius, the patriarch of Constantinople, who had been elevated to preeminence in 471, had profound monophysite leanings. But the further Monophysitism spread, the more determined became Melkite opposition, and in 482 the emperor Zeno made a valiant effort to reconcile the two embattled parties by promulgating an eirenic formula called the *Henoticon*. This document, drawn up, it seems, chiefly by Acacius and his monophysite counterpart in Alexandria, Peter Mongus, anathematised (yet again) both Eutyches and Nestorius, assented to the Nicene–Constantinopolitan Creed and the doctrines of Cyril of Alexandria, condemned every heresy, whether put forward at Chalcedon or any other council, and declared Christ simply to be 'one, not two'. The word 'nature' or 'natures' was carefully avoided. To this document the patriarchs of Constantinople, Alexandria, and Antioch (all pro-Monophysite) duly appended their signatures, and—in theory—the orthodox world was once again united.[16]

In reality, however, the situation was very different. The extreme Monophysites objected to the *Henoticon* because it implied that, contrary to their cherished beliefs, the impure, polluted, and contaminated (the literal meaning of Severus's adjective is 'menstrual'[17]) Council of Chalcedon might possibly have been right; and the latin West objected to it because, not only had Acacius acted without consulting Rome, but the document also suggested that the holy, sainted, and ecumenical Council of Chalcedon—a Council acclaimed and acknowledged by Leo I and all his petrine successors—might possibly have been wrong. The unfortunate result was that in July of 484, Pope Felix III deposed and excommunicated Acacius and thereby instituted the first major breach between east and west, the Acacian Schism, which lasted for more than thirty years. 'Thus', says Alexander Schmemann, 'by trying to preserve the Monophysite East, Constantinople lost the orthodox West'.[18]

By the end of the first decade of the sixth century, the *Henoticon* itself had lost much of its power. It had never been a particularly persuasive instrument of union—compromises never are—and by about 515 Monophysites and Chalcedonians were disputing with each other with just as much vigour as ever and with just as much confidence in the unassailable rightness of their own positions. Nor was the situation improved by the accession to the throne in 527 of the energetic Justinian. In his dream of roman glory he was determined to recover the western parts of his empire which, in the course of the fifth and sixth centuries, had been lost to the barbarian Vandals and the Goths. To achieve this successfully demanded not only military prowess, but also the adoption—at least on the surface—of thoroughly chalcedonian beliefs, since the west, once regained, could not be expected to accept any other doctrine. But to accept the views of Chalcedon for the sake of *political* unity effectively prevented Justinian from achieving his other hope of *religious* unity, and even the pro-monophysite leanings of his wife, the redoubtable Theodora, could not assist materially in the attainment of this coveted end. Justinian's efforts at religious reconciliation[19] were conspicuous by their failure, and they succeeded only in infuriating the western church (which he had just liberated from the barbarians) and hardening the already intractable position of the Monophysite parties. Severus refers to him as an evil man and a heretic, and likens him to Nestorius, but he calls his wife 'the believing princess' and implies—rightly— that her influence on Justinian was considerable.[20] She was, in fact, an outstanding woman, eloquent and learned, and even if the scurrilous tales told by the unreliable Procopius of her supposedly dissolute youth were true, there is no reason why a little early exotic sex should tarnish her remarkable memory.

Justinian died in 565, and the empire which he had reunited—at least politically—immediately began to fall apart once more. The west collapsed, and the war with Persia, which had always loomed on the horizon, erupted anew in about 572. Justinian's immediate successors—the incompetent Justin, who died insane, Tiberius, whose life perhaps ended too soon, Maurice, well-meaning but lacking a sense of judgment and perspective, and the despicable and tyrannical Phocas—were all alike incapable of stemming the persian tide. Their net contribution to the empire was simply to plunge it, by the year 609, into revolution, anarchy, and civil war.[21] From this depressing condition it was rescued by Heraclius, Prefect of Africa, who, having sailed across the Mediterranean to Thessalonika (where he was delayed some months), set out for Constantinople with a great fleet in September 610. Phocas was captured and brought before him, charged with his crimes, and, inevitably, sentenced to death. He was methodically cut to pieces, beginning with his hands and ending with his head. Heraclius was now supreme ruler of the Byzantine empire, and he confirmed his friend and cousin Nicetas (who had already taken Egypt for him as part of his plan of campaign) in the governorship of Alexandria 'or, as it might be called [says Butler], the Viceroyalty of Egypt'.[22] The position, it might be added, was no sinecure. 'Alexandria itself [says Butler again] was as difficult a city to govern as any in the whole world with its motley population of Byzantine Greeks, Greeks born in Egypt, Copts, Syrians, Jews, Arabs, and aliens of all nations'.[23] And the country itself, too long and thin for easy administration, was still rent by the bitter antagonism of Melkite and Monophysite, and plagued by brigandage and the ever-present threat of local insurrection.

Heraclius and Nicetas, however, seem to have been eager to conciliate the Monophysite party. At the time, the alexandrian ecclesiastical hierarchy was predominantly Melkite and Severus tells us that for some years the Monophysite bishops (he calls them, of course, the 'orthodox' bishops) had been unable to enter the city.[24] Under the new administration, the courageous Anastasius, the thirty-sixth (monophysite) patriarch, returned to Alexandria, ordained priests there, and began to build and re-build a number of important churches.[25] Furthermore, on the advice of Nicetas, the emperor appointed as melkite patriarch of Alexandria the saintly and pious John the Almsgiver (John the Merciful, John the Eleemosynary). A remarkable man, revered by both Copt and Greek alike, he sponsored hospitals and shelters for the homeless, demanded honesty in the market-place and justice in the courts, condemned outright the bitterness and disputes which characterised egyptian Christianity, and disbursed the revenues of the patriarchate (which were very considerable) in innumerable acts of charity.[26] Even the appointment of the patriarch Cyrus some years later reflected the same conciliatory tone, but in this case, as we shall see, Heraclius' judgment was grossly at fault, and the consequences of his unfortunate decision were as destructive in the case of Cyrus as they had been constructive in the case of John.

During the period of Heraclius' rise, the Persians, under Chosroes Parviz, had marched into Syria and Palestine. By 610, when Heraclius finally seized power from Phocas, they were within sight of Antioch; in 613 they took Damascus; and in 614-615, they conquered Jerusalem, slaughtered many of its inhabitants, took the patriarch Zacharias into captivity, seized the True Cross, together with other instruments of the Passion, and sent them to Shīrīn, the monophysite christian wife of Chosroes.[27] In the following year, 616, the persian armies were ready to advance on Egypt. Under their general Shahīn (according to Ṭabarī) their advance was rapid and resistance ineffectual. Only the walls of Alexandria repulsed the invaders, who, to wile away the time whilst laying siege to the city, despoiled the hundreds of monasteries in the vicinity and slaughtered their inhabitants. There were six hundred such monasteries, says Severus, with keeps built like dove-cotes (*abrāj al-ḥamām*), and the monks were independent, and insolent without fear, through their great wealth; and they did deeds of mockery. But the army of the Persians surrounded them on the west of the monasteries, and no place of refuge remained for them; and so they were all slain with the sword, except a few of them, who hid themselves, and so were safe. And all that was there of money and furniture was taken as plunder by the Persians; and they wrecked the monasteries, which have remained in ruins to this day.[28]

By 618 Alexandria had fallen (certainly by treason, though the details are unclear[29]), and many of its citizens had perished in the ensuing massacre. The coptic patriarch, Andronicus, was spared, but did not live long after the terrible events he had witnessed,[30] and after the conquest of Alexandria the persian forces turned their attention to Upper Egypt and the final annexation of the whole country. The treatment of the Copts by Chosroes' general was everywhere the same; 'everywhere his path was marked by death and devastation',[31] says Butler, and an old myth that the Copts welcomed the Persians into Egypt as deliverers from the oppressions of the iniquitous Chalcedonians has long been known to be absolute nonsense.[32]

With the fall of Egypt, Heraclius seems to have despaired. He sued for peace with Chosroes, but to no avail, and seemed determined to flee back to Carthage. But then, when his fortunes had reached their nadir, we witness an amazing about-face when, phoenix-like, Heraclius rose from the ashes of his indolence and pusillanimity, seized the reins of power once again, and displayed all the courage and craft, foresight and fearlessness, which had characterised his conquest of the empire at the end of the first decade of the century. For six years he waged war on the Persians and, in a series of masterly campaigns, drove them from Egypt and the Empire. He captured Dastagerd in 628, restored patriarch

Zacharias to Jerusalem, regained the relic of the True Cross, and entered Constantinople in triumph later the same year.[33]

Unfortunately, this astonishing story (which one would not believe were one to read it in a novel) now takes a more dismal turn. Heraclius realised that though Egypt was once again Byzantine, it was still a very turbulent country, and the Melkite/Monophysite conflict, which lurked always just below the surface, could re-explode at any time. He therefore determined, like Zeno before him, to find some eirenic formula which might reconcile the two parties and restore in Egypt some degree of theological and ecclesiastical unanimity. A few years earlier, perhaps in 624, he had held discussions on the matter with monophysite leaders and they had proposed the solution that was later to be termed Monotheletism: the doctrine that although there were two natures in Christ, there was only one energy (*energeia*) or one mode of activity or one operation.[34] These ideas were then refined and elaborated by Sergius, patriarch of Constantinople (whose correspondence with Pope Honorius later led to 'one will' being substituted for 'one operation'), and seized upon gleefully by Heraclius, who immediately appointed as melkite patriarch of Alexandria his friend the metropolitan bishop of Phasis, Cyrus the Colchian (the Caucasian, the Muqawqas)[35] with orders to impose upon Melkite and Monophysite alike the new formula of compromise.

He could not have made a more unfortunate choice. Cyrus had been given jurisdictional as well as ecclesiastical authority —combining in his own person the offices both of governor and patriarch—and his character reflected a mixture of enthusiasm, determination, single-mindedness, double-dealing, cruelty, untrustworthiness, and undoubted courage. It was this complex prelate who, according to Butler,

> was the evil genius who not only wrecked the Emperor's hopes of religious union in Egypt, but who after making himself a name of terror and

loathing to the Copts for ten years, after stamp-
ing out to the best of his power the Coptic belief
by persecution, made Coptic allegiance to Roman
rule impossible; the tyrant who misgoverned the
country into hatred of the Empire, and so prepared
the way for the Arab conquest; and the traitor
who at the critical moment delivered it over by
surrender to the enemy.[36]

Cyrus' early efforts had not lacked success. At a synod in
Alexandria in 633 he had succeeded in reconciling a number
of monophysite groups with the imperial church (they
accepted communion from Cyrus on the third of June in the
chalcedonian cathedral in Alexandria), and he had therefore
reported to Sergius that all was going well. In actuality,
it was not. Despite its subtle presentation, Monotheletism
was, in fact, heretical: it denied, not ontologically but func-
tionally, the presence of a human rational soul in Christ, and
the christian Church had for centuries (ever since the Cappadocian Fathers had condemned Apollinaris) found such a
christology intolerable. Sophronius of Jerusalem, an acute
and learned theologian, spoke against it; Maximus the Confessor, one of the giants of byzantine spirituality and
theology, condemned it; the popes who succeeded Honorius
—Severinus, John IV, Theodore I, and Martin I—all alike
refused to accept it. And with them, of course, went the
whole western church. Despite imperial attempts at silencing
all such critics (Maximus had his tongue torn out and his hand
cut off; Martin I was arrested, smuggled out of Rome and,
after being treated with utmost brutality, ended his days,
cold and starved, in exile in the Crimea), the theological
tide was set against the new doctrine and it could never
have survived for long. In any case, the divisions between
the Melkites and the Monophysites were far too deep to be
reconciled by any compromise, and the most important
leader among the coptic christians—the patriarch Benjamin I
(whom we shall meet in a moment)—had already refused to

deal with Cyrus and had fled Alexandria. To this charismatic and holy man the majority of the Monophysites remained unswervingly loyal, and no amount of subtlety or persuasion could have changed their allegiance.

This did not prevent Cyrus from trying. But when persuasion and threat had both alike failed, then, as W. H. C. Frend rightly says, 'he opened a reign of terror the like of which the Egyptians had not experienced since the Great Persecution [of Diocletian]'.[37] Mēnas (Mīna), Benjamin's brother, was tortured with flaming torches 'until the fat of his body oozed forth and flowed upon the ground',[38] his teeth were knocked out, he was put in a sand-filled sack and taken out to sea, and there, after thrice refusing to acknowledge the Council of Chalcedon (a confession which would have saved him), he was drowned.[39] Samuel of Qalamūn was beaten with raw-hide whips by ten soldiers, and then, when nearly dead, his hands were tied behind his back, he was hung up by one foot and tortured 'until his blood flowed like water' (a common *topos* in the martyrdoms). In the process he lost his right eye, and finally, more dead than alive, he was driven out of his monastery.[40]

Benjamin, meanwhile, was in hiding.[41] A talented and honest man, born of a very rich coptic family, he had entered the monastery of Deir Qibriūs (situated on the coast to the north-east of Alexandria[42]) and there, after his destiny had been revealed to him in a vision, he had been taken by his superior, Theonas, to Alexandria and presented to the then-patriarch, Andronicus, a year before he died.[43] Ordained a priest by Andronicus, he proceeded to live with him, 'assisting him in ecclesiastical works, and in his general administration'.[44] So impressed was Andronicus with the young man that when he himself was dying he nominated Benjamin as his successor, and in January of 626 (probably) his nomination was confirmed by popular consent.[45]

The new patriarch was both respected and loved by the coptic population. He was a stern man but a fair one: a

charismatic leader and a talented organiser. Between 626 and
the appointment of Cyrus in 631, he did much to foster a
sense of unity among the coptic christians and to restore a
sense of dignity to the coptic church. But in 631, in response
to an angelic command (according to Severus[46]), he fled from
Alexandria before the arrival of Cyrus and advised all his
bishops to do the same. He made his way by stages from
Alexandria to Qūṣ in Upper Egypt, settled in a small monastery near the town,[47] and did what he could to govern the
church from there. What he could do, in fact, might have
been considerable, for he had good lines of communication
and his 'flight' from Alexandria had obviously been, not a
spur-of-the-moment decision, but a calculated withdrawal
by a far-sighted prelate well aware of what he was doing.[48]

Cyrus hunted for him without success. Alive and free he
obviously posed a danger as a focus of monophysite sympathies, and it would have been greatly to Cyrus's political
advantage to have him removed from the scene. But for ten
years—the whole term of Cyrus' patriarchate—Benjamin
eluded him, and for the whole of that ten years persecution
raged. 'Stripes, torture, imprisonment and death were the
portion of those who resisted Cyrus and refused to abandon
their belief', says Butler,[49] and the coptic clergy either fled or
were executed. Some went over to the chalcedonian enemy;
others maintained the faith, and were often in grave peril by
so doing. Agathon, for example, who would in time succeed
Benjamin as the thirty-ninth patriarch, continually risked his
life by living in Alexandria in disguise and ministering to the
coptic Christians still dwelling there.[50] This period of blood
and inhumanity—a period which ensured generations of
hatred for Byzantium, the byzantine emperor, and the byzantine church—ended not by any change of heart on the part of
Cyrus, but because in 640 the armies of Islām under
'Amr ibn al-'Āṣ entered the Delta. By September 642 they
had taken Alexandria and, with Alexandria, save for isolated
pockets of resistance, the whole of Egypt. How

had this come about?

Muḥammad had been born in Mecca in about 570. In 610, just as Heraclius achieved the conquest of the Empire and executed the despicable Phocas, he had just begun or was about to begin his ministry. In 618, as Alexandria fell to the Persians, Muḥammad was the leader of a persecuted minority sect in Mecca. In 622, the year in which Heraclius began his great campaign for the recovery of Byzantium, he migrated to Medina, and in 632, a year after Cyrus arrived in Alexandria and Benjamin fled to the desert, God's Messenger died in Medina and bequeathed to his successors an Arabia converted to Islām and an enthusiasm and devotion which manifested themselves in a series of campaigns of incredible efficacy and swiftness. In 633 the remnants of the once great Persian empire fell before Islām; in 634 the muslim forces moved into Palestine and there routed a byzantine army; in 635 Damascus was captured; in 636 the whole of Syria was in muslim hands; and in 637, after a lengthy siege, Jerusalem was surrendered to Khālid ibn al-Walīd by the aged patriarch Sophronius.

It was probably at about this time that ʿAmr ibn al-ʿĀṣ began to plan for the invasion of Egypt, and over the next two years his designs gradually developed and matured. In the autumn of 639, having persuaded the hesitant caliph ʿUmar to give his approval to the enterprise, he set off for al-ʿArīsh, now the capital of the province of North Sinai and then regarded by many as the frontier of Egypt. In 640 he entered the Delta and then, over the next two years, in a series of campaigns which we need not here chronicle in detail, he conquered the whole country and added its wealth and riches to the rapidly expanding muslim empire.[51] How much assistance the invading Arabs received from the Copts is difficult to estimate. That there was some collaboration seems not in doubt (John of Nikiou says specifically that 'after the capture of Fayūm with all its territory', and before ʿAmr had taken Athrīb and Manūf, 'the people began to help the Moslem'[52]), but as Butler points out, this was only after the invasion was well under way, and even then the aid given may well have been 'very partial and limited'.[53] The native Copts may have disliked the Arabs less than the Byzantines, but that is not to say that they ran to meet them, fell on their necks, and kissed them.

On the other hand, the Copts had little to lose by the invasion. They were a subject people in any case, and the question of egyptian independence was never seriously considered. Furthermore, they were Christians, People of the Book (*ahl al-kitāb*) so far as the Muslims were concerned, and the Muslims would therefore extend to them the same tolerance and protection (as *ahl ad-dimma*) that they extended to all people who recognised in the Torah or the Gospel the inspired, though incomplete, teachings of earlier prophets. They would naturally have to pay the general tax, the *kharāj*, and the poll-tax, the *jizyah*, levied on all adult able-bodied Christians who, because of their religion, could not fight with the muslim armies and therefore had to pay for their exemption and their protection in cash, but they could then look for a degree of toleration which, compared with the hideous persecution of the previous decade, would be like exchanging this world for the kingdom of heaven. With the victories of 'Amr the excesses of Cyrus had come to an end, and the triumphant Muslims did not persecute Monophysites.

In 642 the hated Cyrus died (undoubtedly from natural causes, as John of Nikiou says,[54] and not, as we read in Severus, from committing suicide by licking a poisoned signet-ring[55]), and the new Melkite patriarch, Peter, had no authority of consequence. At this point, says Severus, one Sanutius (= Shanūdah/Shenoute), 'the believing duke' (i.e. a monophysite Christian who held the position of *dux* or 'general' in the byzantine army) informed 'Amr of 'the circumstances of that militant [*mujāhid* 'fighting'] father, the patriarch Benjamin, and how he was a fugitive from the Romans [i.e. the Byzantines] through fear of them',[56] and

'Amr immediately promulgated a decree that Benjamin,
wherever he might be, could return to Alexandria in peace
and safety and resume the administration of his church. This
Benjamin did, and after thirteen years in exile (ten under
Cyrus and three during the Arab invasion), the thirty-eighth
patriarch returned in triumph to Alexandria. When 'Amr saw
him, he received him with respect,

> and said to his companions and private friends:
> 'Verily in all the lands of which we have taken
> possession hitherto I have never seen a man of
> God like this man'. For the Father Benjamin was
> beautiful of countenance, excellent in speech, dis-
> coursing with calmness and dignity.
>
> Then 'Amr turned to him, and said to him:
> 'Resume the government of all thy churches and of
> thy people, and administer their affairs. And if
> thou wilt pray for me, that I may go to the West
> and to Pentapolis, and take possession of them, as
> I have of Egypt, and return to thee in safety and
> speedily, I will do for thee all that thou shalt ask
> of me.' Then the holy Benjamin prayed for 'Amr,
> and pronounced an eloquent discourse, which
> made 'Amr and those present with him marvel, and
> which contained words of exhortation and much
> profit for those that heard him; and he revealed
> certain matters to 'Amr, and departed from his
> presence honoured and revered.[57]

The Coptic sun rose again in strength. Churches and religious establishments which had been left empty by the flee-
ing Byzantines were appropriated by the Copts, and the
complex financial administration of the entire country was,
to a large extent, placed in their capable hands. The Arabs
had as yet little experience in running empires and, as
H. Idris Bell points out, they 'naturally took over much of
the machinery of government which they found in the more
advanced provinces which they conquered'.[58] Until the end

of the seventh century most local financial officials were aristocratic coptic Christians (together with a few renegade Byzantines who had stayed on), and, as we shall see, it was quite possible for Copts to achieve positions of very great influence and power in the early years of muslim domination.

During this period Benjamin was able to undertake extensive repair work on the desert monasteries which had been severely damaged during the persian invasion in the early seventh century. The most important of these were the monasteries of Scetis, the Wādī'n-Natrūn, and of these, the most important was the great monastery of St Macarius, Deir Abū Maqar, the seminary, in the literal sense of seedbed, for so many of the coptic patriarchs of Alexandria. The church of Saint Macarius was accordingly rebuilt and consecrated by Benjamin on the 8th Tūbah (= 3 January), probably in 646 or 647.[59] According to Agathon, Benjamin 'was like fire, and his face shone with light'.[60] This is perhaps understandable when we learn what Benjamin had experienced:

> Believe me, my brethren [he said], I have seen to-day the glory of Christ filling this dome; and I beheld with my own sinful eyes the holy palm, the sublime hand of the Lord Jesus Christ, the Saviour, anointing the altarboard of this holy sanctuary. I have witnessed to-day the seraphim and the angels and the archangels, and all the holy hosts of the Most High, praising the Father and the Son and the Holy Ghost in this dome. And I saw the father of the patriarchs and bishops and doctors of the orthodox Church, standing among us here in the midst of the brethren, his sons, with joy,—I mean the Father Macarius the Great.[61]

Benjamin died in advanced old age about 665,[62] and was succeeded by Agathon, his protégé, friend and secretary. In his days the old Melkite/Monophysite rivalry again reared its head, and Agathon was the subject of considerable harassment by the melkite representative in Alexandria, Theodore.[63] In 680 or 681 Agathon was followed, in turn, by John of Sammanūd,[64] and John of Sammanūd by Isaac, the forty-first patriarch and the subject of the biography here presented.

It was during the patriarchate of John, in 685, that 'Abd al-'Azīz was appointed governor of Egypt, and it was under his administration that Isaac lived.[65] He was a remarkable man. The son of Marwān I, the fourth Umayyad caliph, he had been sent to Egypt while his elder brother, 'Abd al-Malik,[66] had been given Damascus. Two very important features mark his administration. First of all, it was the longest period spent by any governor in Egypt between 'Amr and the establishment of the independent Ṭūlūnid dynasty in 868. The caliphate normally allowed egyptian governors no more than two or three years in that coveted post, for the position of the country tempted those with ambition to bid for independence, and its riches could make them all too powerful.[67] Secondly, because he was deliberately excluded from achieving any real power outside Egypt both by Caliph Marwān and by 'Abd al-Malik (who succeeded Marwān), 'Abd al-'Azīz was free to devote his considerable energies to Egypt alone. As a consequence of these two factors combined, he was able to make a real and positive contribution to the welfare and administration of the country. Despite certain lapses,[68] his attitude to the patriarchs and the christian community was, on the whole, favourable. He seems to have enjoyed a good relationship with John,[69] and the *Life of Isaac* implies that between him and Isaac there existed a real friendship. He was certainly tolerant of such christian activities as the construction of churches (he himself, says Severus, loved building and used men like Pharaoh before him[70]). Under his administration Isaac was permitted to restore the church of St Mark in Alexandria and refurbish the patriarchal residence.[71]

The capital of Egypt at this time was Fusṭāṭ, the city

founded by 'Amr after his conquest of the country (for the last eight hundred years it has been no more than a gigantic rubbish dump),[72] and it was here, naturally, that 'Abd al-'Azīz initially established his centre of government. But as a result of flooding and plague in the city and as a consequence of his own health problems (he suffered from a form of leprosy[73]), he moved the capital to Ḥalwān, a much more salubrious spot with thermal springs, lying about fifteen miles south of Cairo. Here, according to Abū Ṣāliḥ, he erected handsome buildings, set up a Nilometer to measure the rise and fall of the Nile, had a large artificial lake dug and a glass pavilion built by the side of it, constructed several mosques, planted trees, and spent, according to one estimate, a million dinārs.[74] Here, too, he permitted Isaac to build a church[75] (and, it seems, two more churches under Isaac's successor Simon[76]). Indeed, according to Abū Ṣāliḥ, 'it was his wish to remove the seat of commerce by land and water to [Ḥulwān] and to depopulate Al-Fustāt'.[77] In this he did not succeed, and his successors moved the capital back again to its earlier location.

In his later years 'Abd al-'Azīz suffered from the jealousy of his brother, 'Abd al-Malik. Marwān had nominated him to succeed 'Abd al-Malik, but the latter intended that the succession should go to his two sons, al-Walīd and Sulaymān. He therefore planned to remove 'Abd al-'Azīz from the governorship and take whatever steps were necessary to ensure that he did not become caliph. What would have happened had he embarked upon this scheme is unknown, for 'Abd al-'Azīz died in May 705 before any real split had occurred, and 'Abd al-Malik followed him in death just five months later.

This, then, was the situation in Egypt at the time of Isaac's accession. It was a country under a relatively tolerant muslim administration, but with a long history of conquest and reconquest, and a deep antipathy to the byzantine state and melkite ecclesiastics. It was staunchly Monophysite,

deeply devoted to its patriarchs in Alexandria, and deter-
minedly opposed to the Council of Chalcedon and all that
that Council represented. Despite its muslim overlords,
much of the financial administration of the country remained in christian hands—'Abd al-'Azīz's two principal
secretaries were two Christians, Isaac and Athanasius[78]—and
it was by no means unusual to find Christians in positions of
considerable influence and importance. After the death of
'Abd al-'Azīz, we might add, this happy situation changed
for the worse. His nephew and successor, 'Abdallāh ibn 'Abd
al-Malik (another son of the caliph 'Abd al-Malik), who succeeded to the governorship in 705, bore down heavily on the
Christians. He forbade them to wear the burnūs, ordered
Arabic, not Coptic, to be used in all public documents, and,
as Stanley Lane-Poole informs us, 'exactions, arbitrary fines,
torture and vexatious passports are recorded, and a system of
badges to be born by monks, by way of licence, was devised:
if a monk were found without the brand, his monastery was
liable to be sacked'.[79] In addition to this, he accepted bribes
and embezzled public funds, and his conduct was so in-
famous that he was recalled by the caliph in 708-709 and
ended his days in ignominy.[80] These depressing events, however, took place more than a decade after Isaac's death and
are therefore outside the realm of our present investigation.

THE DATES OF THE PATRIARCHATE OF ISAAC

There is no doubt that Isaac's patriarchate fell under the
governorship of 'Abd al-'Azīz, but the precise years of his
consecration and death are not easy to determine. Coptic and
Arabic authorities provide conflicting information, and the
arguments in favour of one year or another are fairly
complex.[81] One fixed date, however, seems established by
the statement in Mēna's *Life of Isaac* that the patriarch was
consecrated on the eighth of Choiahk (= 4 December), and

that the eighth of Choiahk was a Sunday.[82] Butler long ago pointed out that the only years in this period when the fourth of December was a Sunday were 684 and 690, and that, since the former was impossible (John of Sammanūd being still very much alive), Isaac must have been consecrated in 690.[83] It is true that this requires us to believe Mēna rather than other writers, but as we shall see in a moment, Mēna was Isaac's contemporary, he came from the same monastery, and he wrote his biography shortly after Isaac's death. It seems to me that details of this nature were much more likely to be kept accurately by contemporary coptic ecclesiastics than by later arabic historians. Nor are we entitled arbitrarily to change Sunday 8th Choiahk to Sunday 9th Choiahk (as does Chaîne[84]) simply to accomodate the date more easily to our own hypotheses. In other words, although it is not absolutely certain, 4 December 690 seems by far the most probable date for Isaac's installation as patriarch.

When, then, did he die? Again according to Mēna, his death occurred on the ninth of Hathōr (= 5 November), but no year is given.[85] All the authorities are agreed that the term of Isaac's patriarchate was somewhere between two years nine months and three years, and this means that his death must have occurred on 5 November 693. If this was indeed the case, he governed the egyptian church for two years and eleven months, which is precisely the duration indicated by Maqrīzī and Qalqashandī.[86] These dates— 4 December 690 to 5 November 693—are accepted by Butler and Porcher, but not by Adolf Jülicher, and since his arguments are important we need to say a word or two about them here.

The problem occurs over the date of consecration of Isaac's successor, Simon I, from the monastery of the Ennaton. According to Severus, he died on 18 July in the year 416 of the era of Diocletian,[87] and 416 of the era of Diocletian is 700 AD (not, unfortunately, 701, as Butler computes it[88]). But Jülicher also accepts the view of Maqrīzī and others

that the duration of Simon's patriarchate was seven years and
a half, and that would mean that he was consecrated in
January 693, ten months before Isaac died![89] Jülicher therefore puts the death of Isaac in 692 (on 29 October, following
Severus,[90] and not 5 November, following Mēna) and then
suggests that 4 December 690 was not the date of his appointment as patriarch, but the date of his *confirmation* as
patriarch. As we shall see in due course, Isaac's election was
not uncontested—certain parties tried to install George of
Sakhā in his place—and it took almost a year before the
problems were resolved. So according to Jülicher, Isaac was
appointed patriarch in 689, confirmed in his position in 690,
and died in 692.[91]

I must admit to having some doubts about this. I think it
much more likely that the duration of Isaac's patriarchate
was calculated from the time of his consecration in December of 690; and, in any case, the dates of the patriarchate of
Simon are not quite as definite as Jülicher suggests. According to Severus, Simon was patriarch for *nine* and a half years
(the Arabic is quite clear and I know of no recorded
variant[92]), and if this were so, and if Simon died in 700, the
entire patriarchate of Isaac is virtually abolished! Personally,
I feel (as did Porcher[93]) that in this welter of chronological
confusion, and in the absence of any undeniable and incon-
trovertible evidence, the safest course is to adopt the dates
provided by the nearest contemporary coptic writer, *viz.*
Isaac's biographer, Mēna, and therefore, for what it is worth,
I align myself with Butler and Porcher and opt for December
690 to November 693 as the most probable dates for the
duration of Isaac's patriarchate.

If, then, he died in or about 693, what can we say with
regard to the date of his birth? Butler, again, points to two
vital pieces of information which provide us with certain
guides in this matter. When Isaac was still a young man, he
wanted to resign his position as secretary in the civil administration to become a monk at Scetis. Since his parents were

opposed to this, he left his post in secret, but after arriving at the monastery of St Macarius he was sent, for his own safety, to Terenouti (the modern Kom Abū Billō, about thirty-four miles northwest of the monastery). There he met the priest Joseph, who was 'a confessor who had been made to stand before the tribunal of the impious Cyrus and had been severely beaten for the confession of the faith'.[94] And at just about the same time, his parents found that he had disappeared; they searched for him in the monasteries without success and then 'went to Alexandria to the archbishop and told him of the matter'.[95]

As Butler points out, if the persecution of Cyrus was over, as is certainly implied in the comment about Joseph, this date must be subsequent to 641; and if there was a coptic archbishop in Alexandria, it must have been after 644, when Benjamin had been restored by 'Amr ibn al-'Āṣ.[96] Furthermore, says Butler, the coptic text continually speaks of Isaac as a 'young boy' when these events were taking place, and this leads him to propose the year 640 (or thereabouts) for Isaac's birth and to suggest that he was about fifty-three—by no means an old man—when he died.[97]

With Butler's first two points I am in agreement. There can be little doubt that Isaac's flight to Scetis took place after 644. But I do not find his third argument equally persuasive since the coptic word used to describe Isaac at this period—*alou*—can mean a 'young man' as well as a 'young boy'.[98] How old is a young man? Perhaps between seventeen and his early twenties, and if this were so, I would be inclined to place the birth of Isaac about a decade before that suggested by Butler. If he were born around 631 or 632, he might have been seventeen or eighteen when he was secretary to Menesōn, and perhaps nineteen or twenty when he fled to the desert. His consecration as patriarch would then have occurred when he was about fifty-eight or fifty-nine, and his death when he was in his early sixties. I am aware, of course, that this is pure speculation, but it seems to me to be a fairly reasonable suggestion.

THE BIOGRAPHY AND THE BIOGRAPHER

According to the information provided in the exordium to the *Life of Isaac,* the author of the work was Mēna, bishop of Pshati. There seems no reason to dispute this. Who, then, was Mēna? Unfortunately, we have little information about him, but he was obviously a cleric of some note since Pshati (or Nikiou or Prosōpis) was one of the most important ecclesiastical centres in Egypt.[99] It lay in the Delta, about eight miles northwest of Minūf/Manūf, and in its day was a flourishing town of great significance, strategically sited, and a strong and well-defended fortress. It had offered resistance to both Persians and Arabs (though not with great success), and was a stronghold of Monophysitism in the days of the persecution of Cyrus.[100] Nowadays nothing is left of its grandeur and its site (which I have visited) is wholly devoid of interest.

The best known of its bishops was John of Nikiou, the author of the invaluable *Chronicle,*[101] but John involved himself in some dubious enterprises and came to a bad end. It was he who, with Gregory of Kaïs and James of Arwāṭ, had tried to save George of Sakhā installed as patriarch instead of Isaac, and under Simon, Isaac's successor, he was made superintendent (*mudabbir*) of the monasteries 'because he was conversant with the life of the monks and knew their rules'.[102] And then (continues Severus),

> some of those who were given up to their appetites took a virgin out of her monastery, and conveyed her to Wadī Habīb [Scetis] and committed sin with her secretly. When this was made known among the monks, there was great distress among them, the like of which had not been heard of in that place. So the bishop [John of Nikiou] took the monk who had committed the sin, and inflicted

a painful beating upon him; and ten days after his punishment that monk died. Then when the affair became known, all the bishops in the land of Egypt assembled in secret and enquired of the bishop what had happened to the monk, so he informed them concerning the event, and confessed that it was he who had beaten him; and therefore they condemned him to be deposed, because he had transgressed the limit of what humanity required in him.[103]

After John's deposition, Mēna was appointed in his place, but apart from learning that he was from the monastery of St Macarius and that he was 'a man held in honour, powerful in words, loving the brethren',[104] we know nothing else about him.

On the other hand, we can hazard a guess as to when he might have been appointed. Simon, Isaac's successor, was consecrated probably in early 694 (or early in 693, if one follows Jülicher), but for three years the *de facto* patriarch was not Simon, but John, formerly *hegoumenos* of the monastery of the Ennaton. The reasons for this, which seem to have involved a power struggle between the cathedral of St Mark and the church of the Angelion in Alexandria, may be read in Severus.[105] Following John's death, Simon took over the patriarchal administration, but was then poisoned by his enemies. Seriously ill for a time, he eventually recovered, and it was only after these events, says Severus, that John of Nikiou was appointed supervisor of the monasteries, beat the monk to death, and was accordingly deposed. His deposition, therefore, can hardly have occurred less than four years after Simon's consecration, and, if Severus is correct, not later than July 700, the date of Simon's death. In other words, and allowing a little leeway for dubious dates, we are looking at the period round about 697-700 for the deposition of John and the accession of Mēna.[106]

According to later coptic tradition, a bishop had to be of

at least middle age before he could be considered for the episcopacy,[107] and although it is always dangerous to read later canons back into an earlier period, it is most improbable that Mēna could have been very much younger. We must remember, too, that Nikiou/Pshati was a bishopric of first importance in Egypt—it is possible that Nikiou and Kaïs had some sort of archidiocesan status in the patriarchate[108] —and it is infinitely unlikely that patriarch and bishops would have appointed an immature youngster to the position. If, then, Mēna were at least forty at the time he succeeded John in the last years of the seventh century, he could have been born no later than about 660, and perhaps a decade or more earlier. In either case, he must have been a contemporary of Isaac, no more than thirty, and quite possibly no less than ten, years his junior. He was therefore a contemporary witness of the events he describes, and although his coptic love of wonder and miracle is clearly evident in his biography, we cannot dismiss his work, as we might otherwise do, simply as 'later hagiography'.

The *Life* is contained in a single manuscript—Vatican Library, Codex Vaticanus Copticus 62—which is a composite manuscript containing sixteen items brought from Egypt (quite probably from the monastery of St Macarius) in the early eighteenth century by Assemani. There are hagiographical works—e.g. lives of Macarius of Scetis and Daniel of Scetis—martyrdoms, an interesting collection of letters of Peter Mongus and Acacius, sermons, encomia, and an apocryphal treatise on the Dormition of the Virgin.[109] The *Life of Isaac* occupies folios 211 to 242ᵛ (ninth-tenth century) and has been edited twice: once by Amélineau in 1890 and again in 1914, in a much superior edition, by Porcher.[110] It is upon this latter edition that the present translation is based.

The other work here presented, the *Martyrdom of St Macrobius,* also attributed to Mēna, appears in another Assemani manuscript—Vatican Library, Codex Vaticanus

Copticus 58—which is a similar composite manuscript to that containing the *Life of Isaac*.[111] The martyrdom or encomium of Macrobius is there the seventh of twelve items (ff. 90-107ᵛ; mid-tenth century), but we will reserve discussion of the nature and authorship of the work for the introduction to our translation of the martyrdom in the second part of this volume.

The *Life of Isaac* is, as Porcher says, a work of edification, not of history.[112] There is no doubt that it was designed for monastic reading (the Vatican manuscript indicates clearly where the lector should begin and end; so, too, does the manuscript of the martyrdom of Macrobius[113]), but as we observed above, the fact that it is hagiography as well as biography is not to deny that it also possesses considerable historical value.[114] It is one of the very few pieces of coptic literature written under foreign domination: we have in addition only the *Life* of Pisentios of Keft/Qifṭ/Qufṭ/Coptos who lived during the Persian conquest;[115] the *Life* of Samuel of Qalamūn, who lived from about 597 to 695, and was therefore an older contemporary of Isaac;[116] and the later *Life* of John of Phanidjōit, the 'new martyr', who was executed under the Ayyūbid caliph Al-ʿĀdil Sayf-ad-Dīn on 29 April 1209.[117]

According to Amélineau, Mēna's *Life of Isaac* provides us with information on four areas:

(i) the internal situation of the coptic church at the time;

(ii) the relations of this church with the Melkites;

(iii) the religious and political relations of the church with the Muslims; and

(iv) the political relations of the conquerors and the conquered people.[118]

He suggests, for example, that the work offers evidence that youngsters needed parental permission to enter a monastery; that patriarchs were in the habit of nominating their own successors, but that elections could be contested and beset by problems; that Nikiou and Kaïs, as we mentioned earlier, might possibly have had metropolitan status under the patriarch; that problems with the Melkites were still quite evident; that early Muslim rule in Egypt was, on the whole, relatively tolerant; that Muslim governors took a real interest in the election of the alexandrian patriarch; that between 'Abd al-'Azīz and Isaac there was a true friendship; that the Muslims retained as much of the previous fiscal administration as possible; that old byzantine titles were in many cases anachronistically preserved; and a considerable number of other details.[119] Many of these matters will be noted in due course; some have been mentioned already and some are rather dubious. Mēna's *Life* certainly substantiates many hypotheses which may be deduced from other sources; and the world and the events he portrays—even though we see them through the stained glass of hagiography—nevertheless offer us a rare and fascinating glimpse into a critical period of egyptian ecclesiastical history which is, as Amélineau rightly says, 'si intéressante, et encore si obscure'.[120]

NOTES

(For a List of Abbreviations the reader is referred to pages v-vi.)

1. For a brief and accurate summary of the history of the christological controversy, see Henry Chadwick, *The Early Church* (Penguin Books, 1967) Chapter 14; for the theological issues, see J. N. D. Kelly, *Early Christian Doctrines* (London, 1968[4]) Chapter 12, and the very useful discussion in Frances Young, *From Nicaea to Chalcedon* (Philadelphia, 1983) Chapter 5 (with an excellent bibliography).

2. See Kelly, 314-315; Young, 236-239.

3. G. R. Driver and L. Hodgson, trs., *Nestorius: The Bazaar of Heracleides* (Oxford, 1925). For bibliographies on this important treatise, see J. Quasten, *Patrology* (Utrecht/Antwerp/Westminster, 1963) 3: 516-517 and Young, *From Nicaea to Chalcedon,* 394-395 (and 230-233).

4. See Kelly, *Early Christian Doctrines,* 319.

5. See Cyril, *Quod Unus Sit Christus* (PG 75:1292D): anyone who uses the terms *phyrmos* ('confusion') or *synkrasis* ('blending, mixture') is a *perittoepēs* (a 'gabbler, blatherer, babbler'—a splendid word!).

6. For Shenoute's views, see D. N. Bell, tr., *Besa: The Life of Shenoute,* 16-17, 78-79, and *idem,* 'Shenoute the Great and the Passion of Christ', *Cistercian Studies* 22 (1987) 291-303.

7. The best account of the council in English is R. V. Sellers, *The Council of Chalcedon: A Historical and Doctrinal Survey* (London, 1953). For Leo's role, see Sellers' index, 357-358 s.v. Leo, Pope.

8. Sellers provides the greek text and an english translation of the essential passage on pp. 131 and 210-211.

9. By far the best account of the Monophysite churches is to be found in A. S. Atiya, *A History of Eastern Christianity* (London, 1967; Notre Dame, 1968).

10. On Dioscorus, see F. Haase, 'Patriarch Dioskur I von Alexandrien nach monophysitischen Quellen', in M. Sdralek, ed., *Kirchengeschichtliche Abhandlungen* VI (1908) 141-233, and the further brief bibliography in *ODCC* 404, *s.v.* Dioscorus. To this must now be added W. H. C. Frend, *The Rise of the Monophysite Movement* (Cambridge, 1972) Chapter 1. The encomium on Macarius of Tkôw, attributed to Dioscorus (but not by him), has recently been published in an excellent edition and translation by D. W. Johnson, *A Panegyric on Macarius, Bishop of Tkôw,* CSCO 41 (Coptic text) and 42 (English translation) (Louvain, 1980). See also *SE* 125; *SAJ* (22)-(24).

11. *HP* (179)-(180). On Severus, see *GCAL* 2:300-318. To Graf's bibliography must now be added F. R. Farag, 'The Technique of Research of a Tenth-Century Christian Arab Writer: Severus ibn al-Muqaffa', *Le Muséon* 86 (1973) 37-66; G. Troupeau, 'Une réfutation des melkites par Sévère Ibn al-Mouqaffa'', in C. Laga *et al.,* eds., *After Chalcedon: Studies in Theology and Church History Offered to Professor Albert van Roey, Orientalia Lovaniensia Analecta* 18 (Louvain, 1985) 371-380; and Sāwirūs ibn al-Muqaffa', ed. K. Samir, *Miṣbāḥ al- 'aql/The Lamp of Understanding* (Arabic only), *Patrimoine Arabe Chrétien* 1 (Jounieh [Lebanon]/Rome, 1978).

12. *HP* (179)-(180). See further the most interesting paper of D. W. Johnson, 'Anti-Chalcedonian Polemics in Coptic Texts, 451-641', in B. A. Pearson and J. E. Goehring, eds., *The Roots of Egyptian Christianity* (Philadelphia, 1986) 216-234; and the important article by W. H. C. Frend, 'Nationalism as a Factor in Anti-Chalcedonian Feeling in Egypt', in S. Mews, ed., *Religion and National Identity,* Studies in Church History 18 (Oxford, 1982) 21-38 (but cf. A. H. M. Jones, 'Were Ancient Heresies National or Social Movements in Disguise?', in *Journal of Theological Studies* N.S. 10 [1959] 280-298).

13. See *HP* (181): a very brief notice.

14. He is commemorated in the *Synaxarium* on 7 Mesōrē (= 31 July [Julian]): see *SE* 276-277; *SAJ* (1252). See further the two very important articles by R. Y. Ebied and L. R. Wickham, 'A Collection of Unpublished Syriac Letters of Timothy Aelurus', *Journal of Theological Studies* 21 (1970) 321-369, and 'Timothy Aelurus: Against the Definition of the Council of Chalcedon', in Laga *et al., After Chalcedon,* 115-166. Ebied and Wickham also demonstrate (*ibid.* 115) that Timothy was Timothy the Weasel, not Timothy the Cat.

15. See *ODCC* 1054, *s.v.* Peter the Fuller.

16. An english translation of the *Henoticon* may be found conveniently in H. Bettenson, *Documents of the Christian Church* (London, 1963²) 123-126.

17. *HP* (181), (189), and elsewhere.

18. A. Schmemann, *The Historical Road of Eastern Orthodoxy* (London/Crestwood, NY, 1963) 141.

19. See Chadwick, *Early Church,* 208-210 for a convenient summary. Further bibliographical references will be found in the *ODCC* 1356, *s.v.* Three Chapters. For a monophysite view of Justinian's efforts, see *HP* (187)-(189). It was Justinian who, in 538, reintroduced the succession of chalcedonian patriarchs in Alexandria, and the Copts hated both his name and his memory.

20. See *HP* (187)-(189). Further on Justinian, see the excellent

account in Frend, *Rise of the Monophysite Movement,* Chapter 7.

21. On these events, see Frend, 316-335, and *ACE,* Chapter 1.

22. *ACE,* 42.

23. *ACE,* 43.

24. Theodosius, the thirty-third patriarch, had been exiled from Alexandria by Justinian; Peter, the thirty-fourth patriarch, governed his flock from the monastery of the Ennaton, nine miles from Alexandria; and Peter's successor, Damian, was at the monastery of Mount Tabor: see *HP* (200)-(214).

25. *HP* (214)-(215).

26. For an english translation (with some omissions) of the *Life of John the Almsgiver,* see E. Dawes and N. H. Baynes, *Three Byzantine Saints* (Oxford, 1948; rpt. Crestwood, 1977) 199-270. The question of authorship, which is somewhat complex, is discussed briefly on pp. 195-196.

27. See *ACE,* Chapters 2-6.

28. *HP* (221).

29. See *ACE,* 75-80.

30. See *HP* (220)-(222); *SAJ* (525)-(526). Andronicus was patriarch probably from 619 to January 626 (see A. Jülicher, 'Die Liste der alexandrinischen Patriarchen im 6. und 7. Jahrhundert', in *Festgabe von Fachgenossen und Freunden Karl Müller* [Tübingen 1922] 7-23).

31. *ACE,* 83.

32. See *ACE,* 87-89.

33. See *ACE,* Chapter 9.

34. On Monotheletism (and Monenergism), see *ODCC,* 917, and the excellent account in J. Pelikan, *The Christian Tradition, 2: The Spirit of Eastern Christendom (600-1700)* (Chicago/London, 1974) 62-75.

35. On Cyrus the Muqawqas, see *ACE,* lxv-lxvii, 508-526; the same writer's *The Treaty of Miṣr in Ṭabarī* (Oxford, 1913; included in *ACE*), 54-83; and P. van Cauwenbergh, *Étude sur les moines d'Égypte depuis le concile de Chalcédoine (451) jusqu'à l'invasion arabe (640)* (Paris, 1914; rpt. Milan, 1973) 91-109. There is no doubt that Cyrus and the Muqawqas were the same person. In the *Life* of Samuel of Qalamūn (see A. Alcock, ed./tr., *The Life of Samuel of Kalamun by Isaac the Presbyter* [Warminster, 1983] 54) he appears in Coptic as *pkauchianos* or *pkauchios* (cf. the reconstructed forms in *ACE,* lxvi). See also F. Nau, 'La politique matrimoniale de Cyrus (le Mocaucas)', *Le Muséon* 45 (1932) 1-17, and A. Alcock, 'Cyrus the Mukaukas and Melkite Patriarch of Alexandria: Un trafiquant de chair blanche?', *Le Muséon* 86 (1973) 73-74.

36. *ACE,* 175.

37. Frend, *Rise of the Monophysite Movement,* 351.

38. *HP* (227).

39. See *HP* (227)-(228).

40. Alcock, *Life of Samuel of Kalamun* 7, §7 (Coptic), 81, §7 (English).

41. On Benjamin, see C. D. G. Müller, 'Benjamin I, 38. Patriarch von Alexandrien', *Le Muséon* 69 (1956) 313-340, and *idem,* 'Neues über Benjamin I, 38. und Agathon, 39. Patriarchen von Alexandrien', *Le Muséon* 72 (1959) 323-347. The first of these two articles is (understandably) heavily dependent on Severus (see his lengthy account of Benjamin in *HP* [223]-[254]; cf. *SAJ* [527]-[530]). Atiya, *History of Eastern Christianity,* 77, n. 1, reports a biography of Benjamin in Arabic by Kāmel S. Nakhla (Cairo, 1946), but I have so far been unable to obtain a copy. See also *GCAL* 1:468-470.

42. See Otto Meinardus, *Christian Egypt: Ancient and Modern* (Cairo, 1977²) 191. According to Meinardus, this was one of the monasteries which had escaped destruction by the Persians.

43. See *HP* (223)-(224).

44. *Ibid.* (225).

45. This is the date as calculated by Jülicher (in his article in n.30 above) and accepted as most likely by Müller, 'Benjamin I', 325. Butler, however, proposes January of 623 (*ACE,* 552), and in this he is followed by Meinardus, *Christian Egypt* 58, and others. O'Leary, in SE 104, suggests 630, which is impossible.

46. *HP* (226).

47. Precisely which monastery is not known (see Müller, 'Benjamin I', 327).

48. See *ibid.,* 326.

49. *ACE,* 188.

50. On Agathon, see *HP* (257)-(264) (cf. *SAJ* [127]-[128]); Müller, 'Neues über Benjamin I . . . und Agathon', *passim;* and R.-G. Coquin, *Livre de la consécration du sanctuaire de Benjamin, Bibliothèque d'études coptes* XIII (Cairo, 1975). For a discussion of the authorship of this last work—it is quite possibly, but not certainly by Agathon—see Coquin's excellent edition, 46-49.

51. The whole story may be read in impeccable English and splendid style in Butler's *Arab Conquest of Egypt.*

52. R. H. Charles, *The Chronicle of John, Coptic Bishop of Nikiu, Text and Translation Society* 3 (London, 1916; rpt. Amsterdam, n.d.) 181 (*cap.* cxiii, 1-2).

53. *ACE,* 211-212.

54. Charles, *Chronicle of John . . . of Nikiu,* 195-196 (cap. cxx, 37),

199 (*cap.* cxx, 67). See also *ACE,* 361-362.

55. *HP* (231).

56. *Ibid.*

57. *HP* (232)-(233) (one hopes that 'Amr had an interpreter). See also Charles, *Chronicle of John . . . of Nikiu,* 200 (*cap.* cxxi, 1-2); Müller, 'Benjamin I', 329-330. Müller, following Jülicher, 'Die Liste der alexandrinischen Patriarchen', 12, suggests that Benjamin must have returned to Alexandria at the end of 643 or the beginning of 644 ('Benjamin I', 330).

58. H. I. Bell, 'The Administration of Egypt Under the 'Umayyad Khalifs', *Byzantinische Zeitschrift* 28 (1928) 279.

59. These are the dates suggested, with good reason, by Coquin, *Livre de la consécration,* 57-59. Other writers, such as Renaudot, Evelyn White, and Müller, prefer a later date (see *ibid.,* 57).

60. *HP* (246); Coquin, *Livre de la consécration* 132-133.

61. *HP* (247); Coquin, *Livre de la consécration* 136-139.

62. See Jülicher, 'Die Liste der alexandrinischen Patriarchen', 11-12.

63. See *HP* (259)-(263). Further on Agathon, see n.50 above.

64. On John, see *HP* (260)-(275); *SE,* 167; and H. G. Evelyn White, *The Monasteries of the Wadi'n-Natrūn* (New York, 1926; rpt. New York, 1973) 1:171-175. Sammanūd is a moderate sized town in the central Delta, lying on the Damietta branch of the Nile (see Amélineau, *Géographie* 411-412).

65. The best account of 'Abd al-'Azīz is U. Rizzitano, ' 'Abd al-'Azīz B. Marwān, Governatore Umayyade d'Egitto', *Atti della Reale Accademia dei Lincei, Rendiconti* Series 8,2 (1941) 321-347.

66. See H. A. R. Gibb *et al., The Encyclopaedia of Islām* (Leiden, 1960 [new ed.]) 1:76-77.

67. For a list of the governors from 640 to 868, together with their periods of administration, see S. Lane-Poole, *A History of Egypt in the Middle Ages* (London, 1936[5]) 45-58. Much more detail may be found in H. F. Wüstenfeld, *Die Statthalter von Aegypten zur Zeit der Chalifen* (Göttingen, 1875-76), but it makes tiresome reading. It must also be remembered that despite its manifest advantages, Egypt was by no means an easy country to administer. 'Amr himself, who certainly knew what he was talking about, is reported by Ibn 'Abd al-Ḥakam (on the authority of Ibn Lahī'a) to have said that governing all Egypt was equivalent to [governing] the caliphate: see C. C. Torre, ed., *The History of the Conquest of Egypt, North Africa and Spain Known as the Futūḥ Miṣr of Ibn 'Abd al-Ḥakam, Yale Oriental Series, Researches* III (New Haven, 1922) 192 lines 17-18 (Arabic only).

68. See *HP* (279) and page 61 below.

69. See *HP* (271)-(274).

70. *HP* (296)-(297).

71. See *HP* (278).

72. Fusṭāṭ (the word means a large tent or pavilion) was built adjacent to the old roman fortress of Babylon (see B, n. 88), which later came to be called Qasr al-Shamaʿah, 'The Castle of the Beacon', and is now generally, though inaccurately, referred to as 'Old Cairo'. In 1168 the city was deliberately burned by the vizier Shāwar to prevent its occupation by Amalric, King of Jerusalem, and his christian soldiers; and although it was reoccupied for a brief period afterwards, it never really recovered and was abandoned after about a century. In the early 1900s Stanley Lane-Poole noted that the traces of Shāwar's fire 'may still be found in the wilderness of sandheaps stretching over miles of buried rubbish on the south side of Cairo' (*History of Egypt in the Middle Ages*, 184), and that was still true when I visited the site in 1985. There is some archaeological investigation underway, but on the whole, visiting Fusṭāṭ (unlike Qasr al-Shamaʿah) is a dirty and depressing experience. See further the *Encyclopaedia of Islām* 2:957-959 *s.v.* Fusṭāṭ (with bibliography).

73. According to Abū Ṣāliḥ (B. T. A. Evetts, ed./tr., and A. J. Butler, *The Churches and Monasteries of Egypt and Some Neighbouring Countries Attributed to Abū Ṣāliḥ, the Armenian* [Oxford, 1895] page 66 of the Arabic text), ʿAbd al-ʿAzīz was suffering from '*dāʾ al-asad*, that is *judām*'. *Dāʾ al-asad* is 'lion-sickness' or leontiasis, and would normally indicate advanced lepromatous leprosy, while *judām* would also normally be translated as 'leprosy', although it may also indicate elephantiasis. Evetts (155) translates the phrase by 'lion-sickness, or elephantiasis'. What, then, was ʿAbd al-ʿAzīz suffering from? Elephantiasis, leontiasis, or leprosy? In fact, there is no confusion at all, and there can be little doubt that what the governor had contracted was Hansen's Disease, which is also called elephantiasis grecorum, leprosy, eastern leprosy, arabian leprosy, and leontiasis. It is an infectious disease caused by Mycobacterium leprae and results in granulomatous lesions and eruptions of the skin and mucous membranes (and eventually of the nervous system and the bones), and those interested may find an illustration of its moderately disfiguring effects in S. Jablonski, *Illustrated Dictionary of Eponymic Syndromes and Diseases* (Philadelphia, 1969) 138.

74. See Abū Ṣāliḥ, *Churches and Monasteries,* 155 (pp. 66-67 of the Arabic text); on Abū Ṣāliḥ, see *GCAL* 2:338-340. See further, Rizzitano, ''Abd al-ʿAzīz B. Marwān', 339-340.

75. See *HP* (278) and page 75 below.

76. See *HP* (296).

77. Abū Ṣāliḥ, *Churches and Monasteries*, 155 (p. 67 of the Arabic text).

78. See B, n. 60.

79. Lane-Poole, *History of Egypt in the Middle Ages*, 27.

80. See the *Encyclopaedia of Islām*, 1:42. Cf. *HP* (308)-(311).

81. For those interested in examining the various arguments in detail, five discussions are essential. In chronological order they are as follows:
(i) E. Amélineau, *Histoire du patriarche copte Isaac, Publications de L'école des lettres d'Alger; Bulletin de correspondance Africaine* II (Paris, 1890) x-xiv;
(ii) Butler's discussion in *ACE*, 548-552 (1902);
(iii) Jülicher, 'Die Liste der alexandrinischen Patriarchen' (1922: see n.30 above);
(iv) M. Chaîne, 'La durée du patriarcat d'Isaac, XLIᵉ Patriarche d'Alexandrie', *Revue de l'Orient Chrétien* 23 (ser. 3,3) (1922-23) 214-216; and
(v) E. Porcher, 'Les dates du patriarcat d'Isaac', *Revue de l'Orient Chrétien* 24 (ser. 3,4) (1924) 219-222. One should also refer to F. Nau's note in E. Porcher, ed./tr., *Vie d'Isaac, Patriarche d'Alexandrie de 686 à 689*, PO 9/3 (#54) (Paris, 1914; rpt. Turnhout, 1974) p. (4): Nau defends the dates 684 to 687, and E. Tisserant and G. Wiet, 'La liste des patriarches d'Alexandrie dans Qalqachandi', *Revue de l'Orient Chrétien* 23 (1922-23) 123-143, though the date given there (p. 134) for Isaac's consecration (the eighteenth year of Justinian = AD 703) is impossible. References to the relevant arabic and coptic authorities will be found in these discussions.

82. See page 64 below.

83. See *ACE*, 548-549.

84. Chaîne, 'La durée du patriarcal d'Isaac', 216.

85. See page 76 below.

86. See F. Wüstenfeld, *Macrizi's Geschichte der Copten* (Göttingen, 1845) 53 (p. 21 of the Arabic text); S. C. Malan, *A Short History of the Copts and of Their Church Translated from the Arabic of Tāqi-ed-Dīn El-Maqrīzī* (London, 1873) 75; Tisserant and Wiet, 'La liste des patriarches . . . dans Qalqachandi', 134. Maqrīzī's notice is very brief: 'After [Agathon] there came Isaac. He was a Jacobite and remained two years and eleven months until he died.' Maqrīzī has omitted John of Sammanūd.

87. See *HP* (300).

88. See *ACE*, 552; Porcher, 'Les dates du patriarcat d'Isaac', 219, 221. For the conversion of E. M. dates to AD dates, see *SE* 34-35, and C, n.10 below.

89. See Jülicher, 'Die Liste der alexandrinischen Patriarchen', 13-14.

90. See *HP* (280), which gives the date of Isaac's death as the second, not the ninth, of Hathōr. I am not sure that Jülicher is being strictly logical here: a few sentences after accepting the *HP* date of 2nd Hathōr, he states that in the case of a conflict between the *HP* and Mēna's biography, the latter 'being contemporary' probably has a better claim to accuracy (p. 14).

91. Jülicher, 14.

92. See *HP* (300).

93. See Porcher, 'Les dates du patriarcat d'Isaac', *passim*.

94. See page 47 below.

95. See page 48 below.

96. See *ACE*, 549-550.

97. *Ibid*.

98. See Crum, *Dictionary*, 5a. The most recent Coptic dictionary, the *Dictionnaire étymologique de la langue copte* of V. Vycichl (Louvain, 1983) 7a, translates *alou* by 'enfant, garçon, jeune homme'.

99. See Amélineau, *Géographie*, 277-283 (Nikīous/Pshati/Niqyūs); A. Calderini, *Dizionario dei Nomi Geografici e Topografici dell'Egitto Greco-Romano* (Cairo/Milan, 1935) III/iv: 358-359 (Nikiou), IV/ii: 194-195 (Prosōpitēs).

100. See *ACE*, 16-17, n.1., and Butler's index, 560, *s.v.* Nikiou.

101. See n.52 above. See further *GCAL* 1:470-472.

102. *HP* (287). In the Ethiopic text of his *Chronicle* the author refers to himself as 'John, *madabber*, bishop (*pappas*) of the town of Nakeyūs' (see H. Zotenberg, ed./tr., *Chronique de Jean, évêque de Nikiou* [Paris, 1883] 221). *Madabber* is obviously the ethiopic spelling of the arabic *mudabbir* 'superintendent, supervisor, manager, director, administrator', and I would suggest, therefore, that the passage should be translated as 'John the superintendent [of the monasteries], bishop of the town of Nikiou'. This is important since it seems to me that Zotenberg (p. 5), and Charles, following him (p. iii), misread the expression and see John not as superintendent of the monasteries, but as superintendent of the other bishops of Upper Egypt: 'He was the Coptic bishop of Nikiu and "rector" [Zotenberg's "recteur"/*Madabber*/*mudabbir*] of the bishops of Upper Egypt who took part in the election of the successor of John of Samnūd in 690 A.D.' (Charles, *Chronicle of John . . . of Nikiu*, iii). As we shall see, there is indeed some evidence that the diocese of Nikiou may have enjoyed some sort of metropolitan status amongst the Upper Egyptian sees (see B, n. 96 below), but in my own view the evidence for this is to be found in places other than the *Chronicle* of bishop John. In any case, according to Severus, it

was Gregory of Kaïs, not John of Nikiou, who was the presiding bishop at the election of John of Sammanūd's successor (see *HP* [276] and B, nn. 83 and 97 below).

103. *HP* (287).

104. *HP* (288).

105. See *HP* (279)-(284).

106. Charles, *Chronicle of John . . . of Nikiu,* iii, gives 696 as the date of John's appointment as 'administrator general of the Monasteries', and Zotenberg, *Chronique de Jean . . . de Nikiou,* 5, suggests, 'vers 694'. Neither offers any substantiating arguments.

107. See O. H. E. KHS-Burmester, *The Egyptian or Coptic Church* (Cairo, 1967) 166-167.

108. See B, n.96 below.

109. For a full and detailed description, see A. Hebbelynck and A. van Lantschoot, *Codices Coptici Vaticani Barberiniani Borgiani Rossiani: I, Codices Coptici Vaticani* (Vatican City, 1937) 432-449.

110. Amélineau, *Histoire;* Porcher, *Vie.* Amélineau earlier presented a detailed paraphrase of Isaac's life in his 'Sur deux documents coptes écrits sous la domination arabe', *Bulletin de l'Institut d'Égypte (Cairo)* ser. 2, vol. 6 (1885) 324-369 (the other document is the martyrdom of John of Phanidjōit: see n. 117 below), and a very brief paraphrase may be found in G. M. Lee, 'Coptic Christianity in a Changing World', in Mews, ed., *Religion and National Identity* (n. 12 above) 39-45. Lee refers to the work as 'a jewel of Coptic literature' (41) and a 'Coptic masterpiece' (45). He also likens Isaac to Cardinal Hume.

111. For a full description, see Hebbelynck and van Lantschoot, *Codices Coptici Vaticani,* 385-399. The text was edited, with a french translation, by Henri Hyvernat in his *Les Actes des martyrs de l'Égypte* (Paris, 1886; rpt. Hildesheim/New York, 1977) 225-246.

112. Porcher, *Vie* (3)-(4).

113. See Hebbelynck and van Lantschoot, *Codices Coptici Vaticani,* 392-393, 445.

114. Tito Orlandi, both in his *Elementi di Lingua e Letteratura Copta* (Milan, 1970) 110, and in his 'Coptic Literature', in Pearson and Goehring, *Roots of Egyptian Christianity* (n. 12 above), 78, refers to the work as an 'important historical document'.

115. There are versions of the *Life of Pisentius* in Sahidic Coptic, Bohairic Coptic, and Arabic: for details, see *SE* 235-236, and *GCAL* 1:465-466. There are english translations of the Sahidic Life (by Budge) and the Arabic Life (by O'Leary), and a French translation of the Bohairic Life (by Amélineau): see *ibid.*

116. The *Life of Samuel* is now available in the edition and

translation of Anthony Alcock (n. 35 above).

117. The bohairic text and a french translation may be found in E. Amélineau, 'Un document copte du XIIIe siècle', *Journal Asiatique* ser. 8, vol. 9 (1887) 113-190 (with important notes and corrections by M. P. Casanova, 'Notes sur un texte copte du XIIIe siècle', *Bulletin de l'Institut français d'archéologie orientale, Cairo* 1 [190] 113-137, and in a better edition in I. Balestri and H. Hyvernat, *Acta Martyrum II,* CSCO 86 (Paris, 1924; rpt. Louvain, 1953) 157-182 (Latin translation by Hyvernat in *Acta Martyrum II* [*versio*], CSCO 125 [Louvain, 1950] 108-125).

118. See Amélineau, *Histoire* ix-x.

119. See *ibid.* ix-xxxvii.

120. *Ibid.* xxxvi.

THE LIFE OF
ISAAC OF ALEXANDRIA

THE LIFE OF THE GREAT AND HOLY
PATRIARCH AND THE ARCHBISHOP OF THE
GREAT CITY OF ALEXANDRIA, ABBA ISAAC,
RELATED BY THE HOLY ABBA MĒNA THE
MOST PIOUS BISHOP OF THE CITY OF
PSHATI.[1] IN THE PEACE OF GOD. AMEN.

THE COMMEMORATION of the honored patriarch,
O my beloved, arouses gladness in my heart; it calls us
today to exult in spiritual joy and enter upon his holy
eulogy. But who could declare the honor of the true
shepherd, the faithful and just high-priest who, from his
childhood, loved virtue and the way of life of the holy
angels, and who, by imitating their way of life, has made
himself like them?

For it was thus that he appeared, so shining in every way
that he was entrusted with tending the sheep of the Church
of the great city of Alexandria, of the whole of Egypt, and
even of all under heaven. I, who am so insignificant, have
the courage to say not one word on my own [authority],
but what we have heard and what we know, these things we
have written down for you, you who read and you who
listen, to the glory of God and of his saints.

This saint, my brothers, was an Egyptian by race and
came from a village called Pisho.[2] His parents were very

pious and had a multitude of goods, men-servants, and maid-servants. It happened that when they had brought forth this holy child they called his name Isaac, the meaning of his name being 'Joy'.[3] When the [right number of] days had passed for him to be baptized in accordance with christian custom,[4] his parents brought him before the bishop of that time, a man filled with the Spirit. When he was immersing the holy child in the font in the name of the Father and of the Son and of the Holy Spirit, the consubstantial Trinity, he opened his eyes and saw a shining cross on the child's head, and as if moved by the Holy Spirit, he cried out in a prophetic voice, saying, 'You are great, Lord God, Ruler of All, and you alone are great, and there is none who will ask us your intentions'.

When the holy bishop had said this, he gave him to his parents, saying, 'Guard this child, for he is a gift of God. He will be a great high-priest in the house of God and many peoples will be entrusted to him'. When his parents heard these things, they raised their voices, saying, 'May the name of the Lord be blessed from eternity to eternity!'

When the holy child had advanced in age his parents took him to school, and in a few days he knew both the value of the letters and all that he was taught.[5] Because of this, all who were at school with him were amazed at him, seeing the knowledge which God had given him, and all who were in the school would bow their heads before him.

When he was filled with knowledge and wisdom, his parents put him into the hands of a relative of theirs whose name was Menesōn. He was registrar[6] to George, the prefect[7] of the land of Egypt, and the young man Isaac was to be secretary[8] to him. While he was in that place he displayed the life of a monk, first committing to heart the psalms, [then] fasting each day until evening, persevering in the worship,[9] and wearing next to the skin[10] a hair-shirt, but over this a splendid garment.

It happened one day that the magistrate[11] called Menesōn

because he wanted him to write an urgent letter—[Menesōn] being the principal secretary—but he did not find him. Straightaway he became enraged with great anger, called the young man Isaac and asked him, 'Where is your master?' He said, 'I do not know'. And when the young man saw him with his face darkened, he spoke to him as holy David [spoke] to the king of Israel, saying, 'Why is my Lord's face darkened? Command me: I will write the letter as you would like it'. The magistrate was astonished at his reply and, to test him, said to him, 'Go into one of these rooms, write it, and bring it for me to see'. So when he had written it, he brought it and showed it to him, and when the magistrate saw the letter which the young man had written, he was utterly amazed. 'So this is what you are like!', the magistrate said, 'And I did not know it until today! Truly, man looks at the face, but God [sees] the heart.[a] And from that day, the magistrate made him the head of all the secretaries.

Everyone cherished him; all who were in the *praetorium*[12] loved him. And because of the wisdom which was in him he was called 'the saint'. His parents, for their part, regarded him as a mirror, hoping that he would become the master of everything they possessed, and they wanted him to take a wife in the hope of seeing his sons. They themselves did not know that his role was not that of Jacob,[13] but that he would be a father to a multitude of sons. But he who had set apart Jeremiah from [the time] he was in the womb [β] had also set apart this saint. Nevertheless, his parents forced him against his will, betrothed him to a woman, and waited for the wedding day. But the young man Isaac had a great desire for the sweet way of life of the monk, for this holy young man remembered the Lord crying out in the Gospel, 'Whoever loves his father and his mother more than me is not worthy of me',[γ] and again, 'He who leaves his father or

a   1 Sam 16:7

β   Jer 1:5

γ   Mt 10:37

mother or wife or sister or brother or house or flock or
children for the kingdom of God will receive a hundredfold
in this age and life eternal in that which is to come',[a] and
again the apostle cried, 'The form of this world will pass
away, but I want you to be without anxiety'.[β] And again
John the apostle says, 'The world with its lust will pass away,
but he who does the will of God will live for ever',[γ] and
again, 'Everything that is in the world—the lust of the eyes
and the lust of the flesh, things unattainable in their retribution[14]—these things are not of God, but of the world'.[δ]
These are what the righteous [man] meditates[15] on day after
day, and he decides within himself to abandon the vanity of
this world and its cares.

While these things were happening, George the prefect,[16]
to whom the young man was secretary, departed the body.
With the death of the magistrate, the saint found the occasion he desired, and he therefore left the *praetorium,* went
to his house and was with his parents for a few days. They
cherished him and comforted him, for they feared that he
would vanish from them since they saw the great ardor he
had for what is good. For his part, after these things had
occurred in this way, the young man Isaac left the house
without letting any of them know.

He went to the holy mountain of Scetis[17] where dwell
choirs of holy angels of God. These are the blessed monks
who, in the sufferings of virtue, crucify their flesh, bearing
in their body every day the death of Jesus in the hope of the
glory which will be revealed to them, as it is written, 'If
we suffer with him, we shall also be glorified with him'.[ε]

When he had gone to Scetis he dwelt in the monastery of

---

a   Mt 19:29, Mk 10:29-30, Lk 18:29-30
β   1 Cor 7:31-32
γ   1 Jn 2:17
δ   1 Jn 2:16
ε   Rom 8:17

abba Zacharias of good memory,[18] the priest and superior[19] of the holy *lavra* of abba Makarios.[20] He [later] became bishop of the city of Saïs,[21] and was a holy man who received[22] revelations. When the old man abba Zacharias saw the holy young man coming towards him, the Lord opened his eyes and he saw the sign of a cross over his head, and when he saw this marvelous sign, he was greatly astonished and cried out, saying, 'As your works are great, O Lord, your thoughts are very deep!'[a] And while the holy old man abba Zacharias was deliberating within himself as to what the young man would become, he suddenly had a vision of an angel of the Lord, saying, 'Behold! the Lord has favored you with a great and holy gift: this is the young man who is coming to you. For he will be a shepherd of the sheep of Christ and patriarch of the bishops'. And when the holy old man had heard these things from the angel, he was very glad.

When [Isaac] had been with the holy old man for three days, he discussed his safety[23] with him. [The old man] straightaway sent him to Terenouti[24] to the house of one of his friends so that he could stay with him until he knew what the young man's parents would do. He was afraid that they would find him with him and would do evil to the holy place on his account, for the old man was a man who was very famous.

When this young man came to Terenouti he went into the man's house, [and] the man's sons said to him, 'Our father has gone to the field'. Then the young man went up to the man's barn, took a bundle of hay,[25] laid it over him and went to sleep. The man then came back from the field. His name was Joseph; he was a priest, and many attested of him that he was a confessor who had been made to stand before the tribunal of the impious Cyrus[26] and had been severely beaten for the confession of the faith. So when the priest came back from the field, he put his donkey in the stable[27]

---

a Ps 92:5

and went up to the barn to give the donkey a bundle of
fodder. He saw the bundle of hay which had been placed on
the young man, bearing upon it the form of a shining cross
which threw out flashes of light. When he saw this marvellous
spectacle, the priest was amazed, and when he came to look
and see the holy young man, he asked him, 'Where are you
from, my son?' [Isaac] explained the matter to him. Straightaway he took the young man's head and kissed it, saying,
'The blessing of the Lord is upon the head of the righteous',[a] and again, 'On their head shall come blessings and
joy'.[β] And the old priest kept him with him for some days.

Let us return to the story on the day that the young man
Isaac went forth from his house, and for the glory of God we
will tell you what happened. When his parents had looked for
him without finding him, there were many tears and great
grief, and their joy became grief for them. When they had
visited all the monasteries without finding him, they went to
Scetis to look for him [there], but the holy old men did
not reveal him to them. For it is their custom for each to
suffer for the others so as to be delivered from the lusts of
the world, putting all their zeal into fulfilling the words of
the Saviour, 'There is no love greater than this, that one lays
down his life for his friend'.[γ]

When his parents saw that [the monks] would not reveal
him to them, they went to Alexandria to the archbishop[28]
and told him of the matter. The archbishop, fearing that they
would inform the [civil] authority[29] and do evil to the holy
place, sent a letter to Scetis so that [Isaac] would not be
allowed west of the river.[30]

When the holy old man abba Zacharias saw the snares of
the devil, he chose to take upon himself a myriad dangers
rather than give him up again to his fleshly [parents, thus]

---

a Pr 10:6
β Is 35:10, 51:11
γ Jn 15:13

fulfilling the word of the Saviour, 'Whoever receives one such child in my name receives me myself'.[a] So when he had shaved the young man's head, he placed upon him the monk's habit. [Then] he called one of his disciples, an ascetic whose name was Abraham, and said to him, 'Arise, take this young man and go to the mountain of Pamaho.[31] Stay there until the Lord persuades his parents [to change their minds],[32] and I will send for you'. They arose and went off, as their father had said to them.

When they had been six months on that mountain,[33] the holy Isaac said to the old man Abraham, 'Arise, come with me to my parents so that I can show myself to them, for truly, if I do not show myself to them, they will not leave me free'. When the old man Abraham heard these [words] of Isaac he was very sad, for he thought that the young man would change his mind[34] and want to leave the monastic life because of the afflictions which had come upon him. Then the old man spoke to him and said, 'Do not be faint-hearted in [the face of] these afflictions, for it is written: "Affliction produces patient endurance; patient endurance, trial; trial, hope; and hope is not confounded".[β] So now, my beloved brother, let us endure [our afflictions] for this short time, for truly is it written, "Those whom the Lord loves, he chastises",[γ] and again it is written, "My son, if you come to serve the Lord, prepare your soul for temptation".[δ] For it is written, "Test me, O God, and know my heart".[ε] If God does not test you at the start, how will he know our love for him?' These and other similar things the holy old man said to him.

The holy young man Isaac answered and said, 'You have

---

a Mt 18:5
β Rom 5:3-5
γ Pr 3:12
δ Sir 2:1
ε Ps 26:2

given me good instruction, O my holy father. I am prepared
not only to follow you, but [also] to die for the name of our
Lord Jesus Christ, for I have left everything behind me to
follow him so that through his goodness I may become
worthy of everlasting life'. When the old man heard these
things from the young man, he was very glad. They they
arose, both of them together, and walked off with each
other, meditating[35] on the words of God, until they arrived
at the young man's village.

Outside the village there was a place [belonging] to his
parents in which dwelt an old monk. When the sun had set
they found lodging in this place, and [the old monk] received them joyfully, although he did not know them. The
young man Isaac asked him, 'My father, do you know
whether Isaac the secretary[36] has been found?' He replied,
'He has not been found, and there is great grief in the young
man's house on his account, for since he went away from
them, they have been grieving'. Then [Isaac] replied, saying,
'I am Isaac', and the old monk was amazed. Afterwards he
venerated him and [Isaac] made him swear that he would
tell no one.

There was a relative of the young man Isaac, a deacon
whose name was Philotheos; he was a man who feared God
and was regarded by all his relatives as a father. When [Isaac]
sent for him, he came to him, and when he saw him he was
very glad. The holy Isaac spoke to him and said, 'If I have
found favor in your presence, then speak for me before my
parents so that they will not obstruct me [any more]'. And
when the deacon had left him, he spoke with his parents, . . .
they swore to him.[37] Then he revealed the matter to them.
When they heard it, they cried out with joy and gladness,[38]
and the whole village came running up together on account
of the young man.

But when his parents saw that he was a monk, they did not
know what they would do. They were amazed, and did not
know what they would say. Indeed, because of the oath

they had sworn to the deacon, they could do nothing at all. And they kept him with them for a month[39] until they had been filled with his beauty, for he was beautiful in appearance, so that one would almost say he was an angel of God.

He spoke with them of things which were useful for their souls, and these are the words he said to them: 'I beseech you, O my parents, do not rest your heart on these unstable riches, and do not pride yourselves in the abundance of your goods, for all these will quickly pass. Moreover, do not let temporal things destroy for you those which are eternal. Let the stomachs of the poor be filled from what is yours'. In this way he left his parents and went [back] to the desert.

It was said of him that when he was sleeping he would often see a shining cherub come and spread its wings over him until he rose from sleep, and then he would see it go up to the heavens. O ineffable graces with which God favors the sons of men! Come and see the honor of this man whom the cherubim overshadowed! It was also said of him that from the day of his birth to [the day] he went to God, no male seed came forth from him,[40] for it is written, 'The angel of the Lord surrounds all who fear him, and he will save them'.[a]

A month after he had gone [to visit] his parents, they granted him his desire. Then he sang with the prophet, saying, 'By my God I will leap over a wall',[β] and again, 'The snare has been broken',[γ] and again, 'Your right hand, O lord, has done mighty deeds'.[δ] And when he went to Scetis, to the holy mountain of God, he spoke the word of the Theologian, 'Give me the desert with Christ',[41] and when his spiritual father saw him, he was very glad.

Henceforth he stayed with the old man abba Zacharias,

---

a   Ps 34:7
β   Ps 18:29
γ   Ps 124:7
δ   Ps 118:16 (see Crum, *Dictionary*, 816a)

helping him in everything he did, as Joshua served Moses, and seeing the way of life[42] of the brothers in the monastery who walked under the protection of the rule,[43] surpassing each other in virtue, as trees laden with fruit. As for the holy Isaac, wonderful were the virtues which were manifested in him so that he surpassed everyone in the monastery. On the one hand he humbled his flesh with the sufferings of ascetic exercises, and again, he was gentle and humble, adorned with all the gifts of the Holy Spirit. He did not sleep long at night—indeed, on Sunday he did not sleep at all—and he would light the fire for the brothers, serving them, spreading out [the bread] before them, making himself like the Saviour, who said, 'The greatest among you shall serve you'.[a] His brothers[44] would come to him, bringing a great quantity of money and clothes, and he would distribute them to the brothers in the monastery.[45] He was a comfort to all the brothers who would come to him to receive encouragement from him.

Their spiritual father gave an order to the brothers in the monastery, saying, 'If Isaac enters the cell of any one of you, stand up until he goes.' But he did not tell [Isaac] of this so that he would not become vain. And when the Lord had told the holy old man what would happen to [Isaac], he gave the order to the brethren, as it is written, 'Will the Lord do something without telling his servants?'[46]

O my beloved, if I should also say of this saint that he was set apart from [the time he was] in the womb, I will not be in error, for I see that the statement is appropriate. When he devoted himself to the [holy] writings there was no problem beyond his power, especially in the discourses of the doctors of the church.

There was an old man on the mountain, a great ascetic, whose virtues were attested by everyone. It happened that when he saw the holy Isaac he said to the brothers who were

---

a Mt 20:26

walking with him, 'Behold an Israelite in whom there is no deceit![a] He will be archbishop of the city of Alexandria and patriarch. He will be great before the Lord and his words will reach the ends of the earth!' When the brothers heard these [words] of the holy old man, they were amazed and glorified God who reveals his mysteries to those who are worthy of them, as it is written, 'Those who have not seen shall see, and those who have heard have not understood'.[β]

The holy Isaac was making progress in all the virtues so that his fame was heard in all the land of Egypt, and there were many who left the world and became monks. One of these was Menesōn, to whom [Isaac] had once been secretary, but when he heard that the saint had renounced the world, he too went and became a monk with him.

Another of them, whose name was Iannē, was of noble lineage and [later] became the saint's companion. He was of the heresy of the accursed[47] who said that since the holy Dioscorus they had not had an archbishop;[48] by this they had divided the churches and become heretics. When he came to [Isaac], he made him a christian[49] and a monk, [and in due course] he, too, became a saint, so that he was made bishop and many peoples were entrusted to him.

These were the first gifts which the holy Isaac brought to the Lord, [but] the wicked devil could not watch the saint making [such] progress in the virtues. [So] it happened that while the saint was asleep at night a demon breathed in his ears, and when he arose from sleep, he was unable to sit down.[50] He told his [spiritual] father of the battle [with the demon, for] he was greatly troubled at heart, and since the old man was not [himself] experienced in this great battle, he sent [the holy Isaac] to the place of a great ascetic who had undergone many sufferings from the demons. And when the old man saw him, the young man told him about the battle. The old man said to him, 'My son, I cannot give you a

---

a Jn 1:47
β Cf. Mk 4:12

command on account of your [spiritual] father, for you are a child of the community. Go back instead to your father's place and do what *he* tells you. I hope in God that you will find relief.' When he came [back], he told his father of the words of the old man. His father answered and said, 'Go and clean the brothers' latrines,[51] and I believe that God will give you relief'; and since he was always pursuing humility, he accepted this instruction[52] peacefully. He remained in these sorts of sufferings for six months, drawing the water for them at night and cleaning the latrines during the night. After this difficult battle which weighed upon him, God favored him with a wealth of healing.[53]

It happened one time that the brothers went to the field for a few pieces of firewood, and after they had finished their task they came back to their dwelling. As they were walking along the road, the holy Isaac stayed behind the brothers picking the fragrant plants on the mountain. When he came upon a fragrant shrub that he wanted to pick, a viper in the middle of it wrapped itself round his hand. When the brothers saw him like this, they cried out, for they thought he would die there and then. Then [Isaac] threw it off and came to no harm. When the brothers saw this amazing thing, they threw themselves to the ground and venerated him.

O my beloved, you see that this holy young man had become an imitator of the apostles and had become like them, as the Lord said to his apostles,[54] 'Whoever keeps my commandments will do all the signs which I have done'.[a]

Now it happened at that time that the archbishop[55] was looking for a wise man to make his *syncellus* and secretary.[56] He was told about the holy Isaac and sent to Scetis for him. [Isaac] went to him because he could not disobey him, and when the archbishop saw him wearing a humble habit, he asked him, 'Are *you* Isaac?' He replied humbly, 'I am.' He

---

a Cf. Jn 14:12

[then] commanded him to write a letter to see if it corresponded to what was heard of him. [The holy Isaac] then wrote the letter, but spoiled it intentionally, thinking that for this reason the archbishop would let him go and not keep him, since he loved solitude. He imitated the prophet David who made himself [appear] mad[57] before Achish, king of Gath, when his servants told him [of him], saying, 'This is David the king, before whom the daughters of Israel sang in choirs: "Saul has smitten thousands; David, tens of thousands".'[a] But he did not get his wish in this way.

When they had seen the letter, those who were attending the archbishop said to him, 'Do we need a man like this?' [But] the archbishop, knowing that he had done this intentionally, said to him, 'All right, go and write like this! But know that you will not leave this place!' [So] when the saint saw that he had not got what he wanted, he wrote again a second letter which was very wonderful. When the archbishop saw it, he was overjoyed, just like the man who found a pearl, of whom it is written in the gospel,[β] and the archbishop cried out, saying, 'As we have heard, so too we have seen!'[γ] And he said to those standing in his entourage, 'Truly, my sons, what we asked for we have obtained by the power of God, for it is a man like this that we need!' Then the young man was distressed, since he did not want to go into the midst of men, and he implored the archbishop many times and, with difficulty, persuaded him to let him go. Nevertheless, he arranged with him to spend one month a year writing the paschal letters,[58] and he [then] left him in peace and gained the desert he loved.

While these things were happening in this way, the bishop of the city of Saïs died. [Zacharias, Isaac's] spiritual father, was appointed and made bishop of the city of Saïs.[59] The

a   1 Sam 21:11
β   Mt 13:45-46
γ   Cf. 1 Jn 1:1

holy Isaac was living in the monastery with his brethren.

It happened once that [Isaac] went to visit [Zacharias] and see him, and when they met each other, they rejoiced. Now there was a man, whose name was [also] Isaac, who was the Secretary in the land of Egypt and very pious.[60] He was from a village called Jebronathēni,[61] and he had great faith in the bishop, the holy abba Zacharias. He went to him and besought him, saying, 'Since the king has sent for me to give him an account of the public funds,[62] I beseech you to pray to the Lord for me to reveal to you what will happen to me in this case, so that I might provide for my household.' The holy bishop answered and said, 'My son, I do not have the ability for this sort of thing, as you think I do.' The man replied, 'I believe that the Lord will give you whatever you ask of him.'

When it was evening, it happened that the bishop said to Isaac, his disciple, 'Let us pray together tonight so that the Lord our God may reveal to us what will happen to this man.' And while the two of them were standing in prayer, behold! the whole room suddenly shone with light, and the old man was unable to bear the light and fell to the ground. But the holy Isaac remained motionless, boldly contemplating[63] the light of the Lord, and the angel told them what would happen to the man. When the bishop got up, he said to the saint, 'Your good works are greater than mine, my son.' He replied humbly, 'It is God and your prayers which have given me the power, my father', for the holy bishop had said, 'It is because of his purity that he has sustained the revelation; for it is written, "Blessed are those who are pure in heart, for they shall see God".'[a] Truly, the word of the Saviour is fulfilled in these saints, that is, 'If two among you agree on earth about anything they ask, it will be done for them by my father who is in the heavens'.[β]

---

a   Mt 5:8
β   Mt 18:19

In this way he left his father and gained the desert he loved, and he was living in the monastery with the brethren. He was an encouragement[64] to them and they looked on him as a mirror, and for them he was like an angel of God, fortifying them and summoning them to the struggle.

It was his custom that when he came to the days of holy Lent[65] he would retire to a little cell outside the monastery and meet no-one. [But] it happened once that abba Abraham and abba George,[66] the great ascetics, paid him a visit, and when they came to him, they laid their thoughts before him and found great profit. But when they looked in his cell and saw nothing but a few loaves and a little salt, they were amazed at his endurance. They asked him, 'Our father, what do you eat these [forty] days?' He replied, 'What the brothers eat.' They said to him, 'We see nothing but bread and salt.' He said to them, 'That is what the brothers eat.' And they implored him, saying, 'Let us bring you a few olives!' But he would not permit them, and said, 'It is fitting for me to receive a few more sufferings than the brothers.' And when they left him, they told everyone about his asceticism, and everyone in the land of Egypt spoke very well of him, in accordance with the word of the holy gospel, 'A city will not be hidden if it is set on a mountain, and one does not light a lamp to put it under a bushel. One puts it on the lampstand instead, so that it will illuminate those who are in the house'.[a] They also tried many times to make him a bishop, but since he wanted to be free from cares, he would flee away, as it is written, 'Be still, and know that I am God.[β]

It happened once, in the days of the holy Lent of our salvation, that the holy Isaac went out to the little cell, as was his custom, and the brothers forgot to bring him any bread. After he had been there without eating for the first day, and

a Mt 5:14-15
β Ps 46:10

the second, and the third, until the fifth day, [then], on the fifth day of his fast, he looked and saw a great flat [loaf] of bread set before him, as if it had just come from the oven. And he arose and prayed, giving thanks to God, took off a small piece of the loaf and ate it. Next day, he took what was left to the monastery and gave it to the brothers, who ate it. The brothers asked him, saying, 'Where did you find this fresh[67] bread?' But he concealed the matter from them, saying. 'It was brought to me from Egypt.' When they asked each other, 'Did one of you take bread to him this week?', they could not find anyone who had taken it to him. They knew immediately that it was God's work, as it is written, 'Behold! those who are my servants will be filled; it is you who shall be hungry. And those who are my servants will drink; it is you who shall thirst'.[a] And again, 'If you obey me, you will eat the good things of the earth'.[β] Does not this prodigy surpass even that of the holy prophet Elijah, when bread was brought to him from heaven by the angel after he had slaughtered the prophets of shame?[γ]

One day it happened that Ōriōn, bishop of Saïs (when he was a reader,[68] and had not [yet] been made bishop), came to him to receive his blessing. It was the week of the Pasch,[69] and it was his custom never to sit down during the Pasch, but to [remain] standing, working with his hands. When he came to him, [the holy Isaac] took the net [which he had] in his hands and worked on it. The young man said to him, 'My father, I want to be a monk, but my father's tears do not permit it.' Then the saint went into a trance[70] for a moment, suddenly stood up, and said to him, 'Ōriōn, it is not possible for you to be a monk.' When the young man heard this word from him, he was afraid, [but Isaac] said to him, 'Do not be afraid, but go and obey your father

---

a   Is 65:13
β   Is 1:19
γ   1 Kgs 19:1-8

until he dies. He who spoke with me just now told me that after your father's death you must enter a high office.' He meant [by this] the episcopate, of which [Orion] became worthy. When the young man had heard these things from the saint, he left him and went to his house in peace, glorifying God, as it is written, 'The spirits of the prophets are subject to the prophets'.[a]

After these things, his spiritual father, abba Zacharias, the holy bishop, fell ill with the illness from which he would die. And since God had already told him [of this], he went to his monastery and the holy Isaac attended him in his illness. When he was about to die, he called all his sons, like the patriarch Jacob,[β] and when he had blessed them all, he said to the holy Isaac, 'My son, if you are raised [to high rank], remember your brothers.' By saying this, he signified the grace which would come upon him. When he had finished instructing his sons, he gave his spirit into the hands of the Lord, and sitting around him were great saints of Scetis. When they buried him with great honor, they laid him near his fathers, and also commemorated him and the wonders he had done during his life.

They said of him that he had a disciple who had weak sight.[71] When he went to the old man, he laid his hands on his head and straightaway he could see. He glorified God [and] remained under his father's authority until the day of his death. [This brother] also had a relative in the world who happened to come to this same disease—that is, blindness— and when he heard of it, he was very sad. When he sent for [his relative], he came to him to the mountain of Scetis, and the brother who could see [again] went to the holy old man and besought him, saying, 'Just as God and you had pity on me, have pity on my brother.' When the holy old man saw them both weeping, he was very sad at heart, and after he had

---

a   1 Cor 14:32
β   Cf. Gen 49:1

given them [a taste] of the holy mysteries, he took the cloth with which he held the chalice and wiped it over the man's face. At that very moment he could see, as if he had never been ill, and he threw himself down, venerated him, and went to his house glorifying God who works these wonders.

There was also living in the city of Saïs a man whose name was George. He was a strong young man. The devil made him fall into sin, but no-one knew save God alone, who knows both things hidden and things manifest, and God immediately took vengeance on him, as it is written in [the psalms of] David, 'The sinner has been caught in the works of his [own] hands'.[a] And when they arose in the morning they found the young man lying stiff as a corpse. His parents picked him up and brought him to the dwelling of the holy bishop abba Zacharias. When they met him, they threw themselves down and venerated him, weeping and saying, 'We beseech your holiness to pray to the Lord for our son so that he may be cured.' When he asked them what had happened to him, they said, 'We do not know', [but] God had already told him before they came to him. Straightaway he arose, prayed over him, and he was cured immediately, as if he had never been ill. The bishop said to him, 'Guard yourself from the sin which you have committed. Do not do it again so that this evil will not come upon you [a second time].' But when his parents heard these things, they were amazed at what he had said, for they did not know the things their son had done, and they besought the holy old man, saying, 'We will guard everything you have said to us.' [Then] they left him, glorifying God. And everyone honored him, giving glory to him as to the holy apostles of Christ.

A month after his father died, it happened that Isaac was very sad at heart because of [Zacharias'] parting from this vain world. Then the holy archbishop, abba John,[72] prayed God to reveal who would be worthy to come after him and

---

a Ps 9:16

watch over the holy church. He had a revelation in a vision in which he was told, 'Send to Scetis, to the monastery of abba Zacharias, for the ascetic monk Isaac: it is he who will be your successor.' As soon as he arose in the morning, he sent for him, and when he came to him, he did not let him leave until the day of his death.

It happened in those days that the king sent for the archbishop to meet with him. Indeed, he used to do this very often, bringing the archbishop to him because of the affection he had for him.[73] The name of that king was 'Abd al-'Azīz,[74] and he was also called the Emir.[75] As secretaries he had two pious men—Athanasius and Isaac,[76] together with their sons—and the *praetorium*[77] was full of christians. In fact, when he first came to Egypt, he had tried to do evil to the churches—he had broken the crosses and done great evil to the archbishop[78]—but God, who had punished Pharaoh of old, also put fear into this other in a dream, saying, 'Be careful how you treat the archbishop',[79] and he came to love him as an angel of God.

Now it happened that while the archbishop was there, he fell ill with the illness from which he was to die,[80] and when the magistrates heard, they all came to him to visit him and receive his blessing. They found him in great pain, and when the king had been told of it, he let him leave. When he came to Alexandria, he died, and they laid his body in the church of Saint Mark which he had built.[81] He had said that Isaac should be put in his place, as he had been told by the Lord.

There was, however, a deacon called George[82] who coveted the highpriesthood contrary to the will of God, by whom [alone] kings are made kings, and he persuaded the bishops who had come together there[83] to give him the archiepiscopate, but straightway he received the punishment of his iniquity. For when they had made him a priest, they placed upon him the stole, thinking that they would make him archbishop in the middle of the week, and wishing [thereby] to perform an act contrary to the canons.[84] Straightaway the archdeacon[85] cried out from the altar, as if moved by God, 'It shall not be done in this way! [We must not] perform an act contrary to the canons! Let us wait until Sunday instead!' In this way the Lord prevented him from ever being consecrated, as it is written, 'A man of blood and guile is abhorred by the Lord'.[a]

And on that day the great bishops came to Alexandria, for they had heard that the archbishop was dead and wanted to serve him whom Christ had chosen, that is, the holy Isaac. But when they found that the others who happened to be there[86] were in agreement with George, there was a division among them. Straightaway the messengers of the king[87] came to Alexandria to lead the bishops to him so that he would know whom they would raise [to the archiepiscopate], and when they arrived at Babylon,[88] the holy Isaac served George without thinking of anything like this. [But] in their investigation of George's life, they found many causes [for complaint] relating to him, above all that he was a married man and also had some very wicked children.[89] In this way he was put to shame, and they decided to appoint him whom God had chosen, that is, the holy Isaac.

On the day of holy Sunday, when all the bishops, together with a crowd of the people of Babylon, Alexandria, and the whole country were assembled in the church of St Sergius,[90] it happened that the holy Isaac also came in, wearing a humble habit. And while he was praying, behold! the lamp suddenly broke over him and bathed him all over [with oil]. At once the crowd cried out, 'Worthy, worthy, worthy! The thirteenth apostle! Isaac the archbishop!' And straightaway the bishops and the magistrates seized him and took him into the sanctuary, saying, 'This is the new David!'

On that day, the pious magistrate Lord Isaac the Secretary[91] gave a great feast for the bishops and the clerics, and the bishops seized the holy Isaac and seated him above

---

a Ps 5:6

them[92] against his will, saying to him, 'It is the Holy Spirit who summons you; it is the Holy Spirit who consecrates you, as it is written, "God, our God, has annointed you with an oil of joy from among all your companions".'[a]

The next day they revealed the matter to the king and told him everything that had happened. He ordered the two of them [−Isaac and George−] to be brought before him, and when they were standing in his presence he saw that George was wearing the habit of his priesthood, and the holy Isaac himself was wearing the humble habit of the monks. He said to the bishops and the crowd, 'Which of these two do you want?' They all cried, 'This monk! It is he who is our father!' He said to them, 'He is a man of no consequence!'[93] Straightaway the bishops and the magistrates cried out all the more, 'He is a prophet of God! A pure virgin from his childhood!'[94] But George was saying to him, 'Give me the throne; I will give you riches.' When the bishops and the crowd heard [this], they cursed him, saying, 'May you and your money go to perdition, for you wish to obtain the gift of God with riches!'[β] In this way the bishops utterly excluded him from the priesthood, and that which is written was fulfilled upon him: 'He has scooped out a pit and has dug it: he shall fall into the hole which he has made'.[γ] And again, 'He who exalts himself will be humbled, and he who humbles himself will be exalted'.[δ]

In this way, by the election of God and the consent of the people, the holy Isaac was brought to glory and honor and was consecrated archbishop. Oh, what joy and gladness there was in all the land of Egypt! The crowds went in companies[95] before him, each village changing with the next, to the east and the west of the river, from Babylon to Alexandria. With

---

a Ps 45:7
β Ac 8:20
γ Ps 7:15
δ Lk 14:11, 18:14

him walked crowds of bishops who had all gathered together
to set him over the churches. Among them was John, bishop
of Pshati, who represented the episcopate of the upper
[part of the] country,[96] a man wholly accomplished in the
wisdom of God and of men, and also Gregory, bishop of
Kaïs,[97] who himself represented the bishops of the lower
[part of the] country, and also all the [other] bishops. And
it happened that when they reached the city of Alexandria,
the whole multitude came out to meet him,[98] the clerics
carrying the gospels and crosses, sweet-smelling censers and
burning tapers, and they sang psalms before him until they
brought him into the city. Thus was he consecrated archbishop on Sunday, the eighth of Choiak,[99] and was installed
upon the apostolic throne of the holy evangelist Mark—[he
who was] the lamp which shone upon us—and the service of
[consecration to] the high-priesthood was completed[100]
according to the apostolic canons.

When he had received from God the power of binding and
loosing, he shone upon the whole world. For those in the
episcopal palace he laid down a rule that the brothers would
live in tranquillity[101] in their cell and meditate[102] on the
holy scriptures, and also perform their worship[103] together.
He spoke with them many times and made them envy the
life of those at Scetis.

When the other bishops and the monks of the monasteries
heard that the holy Isaac was archbishop, they came to him
and prostrated themselves before him, for they knew of his
great wisdom and his asceticism, and for them he was a model
for good works. To this saint, then, O my beloved, God
granted the grace of curing all manner of things. Every time
he went up to the altar to offer [the eucharistic sacrifice],
from the moment he began the holy *anaphora*[104] his eyes
would pour forth tears until he had completed the service.
And when he arrived at the moment that the Holy Spirit
came upon the altar,[105] he would see the Holy Spirit coming
upon the sacrifice and changing the bread and the chalice into

the divine body of Christ. While seeing this great revelation, this saint would be seized by both fear and joy. Straightaway his face would send forth such beams of light that everyone was amazed, saying, 'God has made us worthy of such a holy saint!'

His understanding was illumined with regard to the holy teachings, just like the great Athanasius[106] and the wise Cyril,[107] whose successor he was. And when the holy Isaac went into Egypt, he brought back a multitude from their heresies and led them into the right faith of our Lord Jesus Christ. Some he baptized; others he took to himself while they themselves anathematized their heresies by means of the grace with which God had favored him and by his words which saved souls. And when God brought him to a village called Psanasho,[108] he baptized a multitude in that place, both men and women, both great and small.

It happened [once] that at the time of the morning meal, when he was at table[109] with the bishops who were with him, they brought in a man in great torment. His insides were so enflamed that if he drank a cup of water, it was as if he had drunk none at all because of the great fire inside him. When they brought him to [the holy Isaac], he raised his eyes to heaven and groaned, saying, 'You are just, Lord, and all your judgments are right'.[a] The holy patriarch took a cup of wine, signed it in the name of the Father, the Son, and the Holy Spirit, and gave it to the man, who drank it. At that moment, the fire inside the man was quenched; he was immediately relieved and went to his house glorifying God and the saint.

Athanasius the Secretary, of whom we have spoken earlier,[110] was causing this saint distress, for truly, the power lay in his hands,[111] and the old man would lay his concern before God. Straightaway [Athanasius] received from the Lord a reproof for his infidelity, for God sent such a sickness

---

a   Tbt 3:2

upon his eldest son that he was close to death. His father brought in a host of physicians, but he was not cured: on the contrary, he was coming closer to perishing. Athanasius was very down at heart and sought relief for his son, but found none. In [the midst of] all these things, he was utterly distracted,[112] and around him were sitting all the magistrates of the city.

But it happened that night that the Lord sent a revelation to the archbishop: 'Send [a message] tomorrow to Athanasius the secretary. Say this to him: "If you believe in Christ who installed me over his holy church, then the Lord will grant the cure to your son".' When the saint recovered from[113] the revelation, he called his disciple and said, 'Is there a bishop here?' He said to him, 'Yes, abba George is here, and abba Gregory, and abba Piamot, the bishop of Damietta'.[114] The patriarch called the bishops and told them what he had seen in the revelation. Abba Gregory answered and said, 'You know that this man is angry with your holiness. Could this revelation have been an illusion, so that the message is not the truth and will do us harm?' The archbishop, knowing what [had passed] between God and himself, said in reply, 'What I have said to you, say with confidence before everyone! It is saint Mark, the holy evangelist, who commands you!'

When they went, as he had said, they came to the house of Athanasius and found him weeping for his son, and they said to him what the archbishop had said to them. Athanasius answered and said, 'Truly, if the cure comes to my son through the archbishop, I will believe in him as in Athanasius, Cyril, Ignatius, and Severus!'[115] Then Athanasius and his wife threw themselves down at the bishops' feet, saying, 'We beseech you to entreat the archbishop to pray to God for [our son] so that he might be saved, for truly, we ourselves cannot look upon him because of the evils we have done him.' And when the bishops had gone, they told the holy patriarch what Athanasius had said.

Then the archbishop went to the place where the young man was, stood over him, prayed over him, and signed him with his holy hand. At once the young man leaped out of bed as if he had never been ill, and [the archbishop] said that they should bring him something to eat, for truly, he had tasted nothing since the day he had fallen ill. When Athanasius and his wife saw the cure which had come to their son through the archbishop, they threw themselves on their faces at his feet and asked his forgiveness. The archbishop said to Athanasius, 'From this day, my son, take care that you do not do evil to the Church, for he who opposes the Church opposes Christ.' And from that day the archbishop was honored by Athanasius who honored him as an angel of God. And while they were on such good terms with each other,[116] the archbishop spoke with Athanasius about the *Evangelium* in Alexandria[117] so that he would take an interest in it, for it was ready to fall down on account of its great age, and by the grace of God he rebuilt it and adorned it with great beauty. It was also in his days that the [Council of] One Hundred[118] was reunited at Alexandria, for none of the archbishops before him had been able to do this because of the enemies of our faith.[119]

God also kept him safe before the king of the Saracens,[120] who honored him greatly because [the king] himself was honored by him. He would often call [Isaac] to him so that they could sit together and talk, for the king had seen multitudes of cures at his hands.

It happened once, when our father was at worship, that the king came passing by with his whole entourage. He came outside the door of the church, looked in, and saw the archbishop standing at the altar. There was a flame surrounding him and a shining power was behind him, giving him strength. When the king saw this great revelation, he was amazed, and said to one of those who were walking with him: 'Go and call the archbishop to me', for he wanted to know about the power which surrounded him and what it was that was speaking with him in the place where he was standing. But when he wanted to send the man inside, the king saw the power coming forth upon him. Fear seized him and he fled quickly with those who were with him, [though] none but the king himself had seen the revelation. When he went into his house, he lay down in fear; he was like a corpse, and for all that day he was unable to speak. The secretaries came and went in to him to visit him, [and] they found him lying down, sick with fear. When they asked him about the cause of his illness, he revealed to them what his eyes had seen, and when they heard it they were astonished and glorified God.

He sent one of them to call the archbishop, and when he came to him, [the king] asked him, saying, 'At the time you were standing at the altar, who was it you spoke to at that time? And what was it that I saw standing beside you, shining and fiery?' The holy archbishop answered and said to the king, 'I was speaking to my God,' for the archbishop was not ignorant of the power which attended him every time he went up to the altar, just as it had also [done] on this occasion. The king said to him again, 'Do you see your God every time you go up to the altar?' The archbishop said, 'Yes.' Then the king was amazed and said to the archbishop, 'You have great faith, you christians! Until today I thought that abba John,[121] who was before you, was great before God, but now I know that you are his father and higher than he before God.' And from that day, he was a prophet in the eyes of the king,[122] who would always call him 'Patriarch' and take him everywhere he went. But the saint was grieved that he would not let him settle in his episcopal palace, for he always loved solitude.

One day, when the king was in the town of Alban,[123] which he had built not long before in the days of his reign, it happened that he called the archbishop, took his hand, and brought him into his palace,[124] without letting any one of those who waited upon him come in with him. He took him

into one of his chambers and left him alone, and the king
went into his own place. But the king's wife saw great bands
of angels in the chamber with the holy archbishop, and she
also saw a great light, just like flaming lamps. [The angels]
were wearing white garments, and the holy patriarch Isaac
was in the midst of them, and they were praising God all
night in accordance with the custom of the christians. As
soon as it became light she told the king what she had seen,
and said to him, 'After what I have seen and heard, it will
take only a little more to frighten me to death!' And the king
was in great amazement after he had heard these things from
his wife. Then the king said to her, 'I took him into the
chamber on his own so that he might pray for us and our
children', but she swore an oath to him, saying, 'I saw a great
multitude gathered round this old man speaking to their God
in their prayer!' Then, the next day, he let him leave. The
king honored him and the king built churches and monasteries for monks around his city, for he loved the christians.

It happened in those days that a respected man, who was
a christian in his religion, came from the land of the Saracens.
He had two sons: in one there was a demonic spirit; and the
other, wishing to deny the faith of Christ, had fled to
Egypt since he could not do this in his own country for fear
of his father, who was a perfect christian.

After his father had sought him without finding him, he
arose and came to Egypt to get him. He found him having
denied his faith and having chosen the part of Judas rather
than Christ. The father of the young man had also brought
to Egypt the younger son—the one who had in him the
demonic spirit—so that the bishops of Egypt might pray
over him for his salvation, for he had heard that they were
saints of God.

When this christian man came to Egypt, 'Abd al-'Azīz
received him with great joy, for he was one of his relatives.
When he asked him why he had come to him, he told him
everything he had come for, and ['Abd al-'Azīz] received

him with great gladness and great honor. [But] when the man saw that his son would not listen to him and return [to the christian faith], he wept in great distress and said, 'May your blood be upon your own head, my son; from this moment you are a stranger to me in this world and in [the world] to come!'

When he was looking for a holy bishop who would pray for the young man, he came across a false bishop there who was of the heresy of the Acephalites,[125] but since [the man] had been told that he was a bishop, he did not know that he was a heretic. He [therefore] brought his son to him so that he would pray over him so that he might be saved, but when that impious bishop did this, he could not cure him. Instead, the evil spirit tormented the young man and gave him no rest.

The man was in great distress, and when the king saw him with his face saddened, he said to him, 'What has happened to you?' The man then told him the cause of it, and when the king asked him, 'Who is that bishop?', he told him that it was [the bishop] of Nioubershenoufi.[126] The man was grieved when he was told that he was a heretic. Then the king sent at once for the holy patriarch Isaac to be brought to him, and when he had come to the king, he told him about the young man who was ill and why his father was grieved on his account. [The holy Isaac] took a little oil, prayed over it, and anointed the young man, saying, 'In the name of my Lord Jesus Christ, grant your servant healing!' At once the demon came out of him in the form of a flame of fire, and all those who saw were astonished and glorified God. The man immediately arose, threw himself to the ground at the feet of the archbishop, venerated him, and gave him choice perfumes which he had brought from his own country.

The patriarch spoke great words to him on the strength of his[127] faith in Jesus Christ and the salvation of his soul, and the pious man besought the archbishop to write for him the gospel according to John and prayed him for some blessed bread,[128] asking from the archbishop a blessing so that it would be a protection for him all his days. Then he left him, glorifying God. [All this] was in accordance with what our good Saviour had said, 'Whoever loves me shall be beloved of my father, and I myself shall dwell within him'.[a]

After these things, some Saracens who hated our faith went to the king and accused the archbishop, saying, 'Behold! you honor Isaac and receive him to yourself, but he abominates both us and our faith.' The king said to them, 'I myself do love him, for I know by his works that he is a man of God and is obedient to us. The words that you speak are lies.' But they said to him, 'If you want to know that he hates both us and our faith and that the words we have spoken to you are truths, then have him eat with you from the [same] dish and the food that is on it, without making [the sign of] the cross. If he does not make it, then know that all the things we have said to you are lies.' The king answered and said to them, 'I will satisfy[129] you in this matter.'

Straightaway he called the secretaries[130] and said to them, 'I want the patriarch to agree to eat with me, if he loves me, without making [the sign of] the cross.' The two secretaries answered and said to the king, 'We christians cannot eat until we first make the cross. If you let the archbishop first make the cross over the food, then he will eat with you and satisfy you; if you do not let him [do so], then we do not think he will eat with you.' The king replied to them angrily, 'I will have him eat with me and I will not allow him to make the cross. If he does so, I shall kill him!' And because of his anger they were unable to answer him, and said nothing.

So one day, when the archbishop came to visit the king, as was his custom, it happened that he was sitting with the king, his whole entourage,[131] the most important Saracens, and a multitude of Egyptian magistrates. When the archbishop was seated, they brought before the king a basket of magnificent dates. The king ordered the archbishop to eat

---

a Jn 14:23

first, but the saint was wise in the things of God and of men,
and on him the Holy Spirit rested, just as on the prophet
Daniel. Straightaway he stretched out his right hand, cleverly
took the basket on which were the dates, and said to the king,
'From which place would you like me to eat? This place or
that place? Here or there?' The king did not know what the
archbishop had done, but the secretaries and magistrates
understood what he had done and were amazed at his great
intelligence and the incredible gifts with which God had
favored him.

The king answered and said to him, 'Eat from whichever
part you want', and when they had finished eating the dates,
the king let the archbishop leave. The king said to the
secretaries and magistrates, as if congratulating himself,
'I made him eat without [making the sign of] the cross!'
They said to him joyfully, 'He did not eat until he had first
made the cross!' The king said to them, 'In what way did he
make the cross?' They said to him, 'When he put forth his
finger to the four parts of the basket saying: "Would you like
me to eat in this place or that? In that place or this?": it was
at that moment that he made the cross over the dates'. Then
the king was amazed and said, 'Truly, I have never found
a man as wise as he!'

God, who gave glory and grace to the prophet Daniel
before the kings of the Chaldeans and the Persians, also
glorified this saint before the king of the Saracens. And [the
king], too, glorified him, always calling him 'Patriarch' because of the grace of God which was in him.

Listen, and I will tell you another marvel! It happened at
that time that the king of Makouria sent messengers to the
archbishop with letters telling him how the bishops in his
country had become few [in number] because of the length
of the journey and the time [it took to travel there from
Egypt], for by [order of] the king of Maurōtania, they
could not pass through there until peace had been made

with him.[132] Although the two kings established in these
countries were both christians, they had not made peace with
each other, for while one of them—the king of Maurōtania—
was at peace with the king of the Saracens, the other—the
[king] of the great country of Makouria—had not made
peace with the king of the Saracens.

It happened that when the archbishop read the king's
letters and knew what was in them, he was greatly distressed
on behalf of the churches, and he immediately wrote letters
to the king of Maurōtania, giving him counsel and instruction
through the words of the holy Scripture, saying in addition,
'Both of you are christians!' After he had written many words
to him to establish his soul in the orthodox faith of the Son
of God, he then also wrote to him [to tell him] not to prevent
the men of the upper kingdom from passing through his
country when they were going on their bishop's business so
that the churches should not be deserted. ['Otherwise', he
said,] 'you will find yourself in great disgrace before God!'

When the enemies of our faith knew of these things, they
slandered the archbishop before the king, saying, 'We tell
you, O king, that the king of Makouria has sent messengers
with letters to abba Isaac the archbishop so that he will appoint a bishop for them whom they may take [back] to their
own country. And not only this, but he has also sent [a
message] to the king of Maurōtania counselling him to make
peace with our enemy, the king of Makouria. If this happens,
O king, they will be of one mind, and will rise up against us
and make war on us.'

When the king heard these things, he was very angry, and
immediately sent messengers to Alexandria with letters for
the governor[133] written in these terms: 'As soon as these
letters reach you, seize the archbishop and send him to me
with [all] speed.' The king had resolved in his heart that as
soon as [the archbishop] reached him, he would take off his
head with the sword.

When the letters of the king arrived, they found the holy

archbishop assembled [with his congregation] in the church, for it was the week of the saving Pasch of Christ.[134] Oh! how great was the sorrow and the anguish which occurred on that day! Not just among those of our faith, but also with all those who knew of his great intimacy[135] with God! All were in sorrow for their shepherd, for they did not know what he had been accused of before the king. But [the messengers] quickly set him on [his donkey] and took him to Babylon to put him to death.

As the holy archbishop was sitting on the donkey going through the streets of Babylon, it happened that the whole multitude walked with him, as was the custom, until they knew what would happen to their shepherd. And when he came walking in to the king, he saw two tall men wearing white garments, and no fleshly tongue could speak of their glory and honor. He saw them walking with him, one on his right hand and one on his left, and they were saying to him, 'Do not be afraid, faithful patriarch; behold! we walk with you and no evil will befall you!' He asked them, 'And you, who are in such great glory, who are you?' The one on the right, whose appearance was that of an old man, answered and said to him, 'I am Cephas who is called Peter; this other is Mark, my true son. From the day you were seated on the high-priestly throne, we have been with you wherever you go. Have courage, and do not be afraid. Since this year you will end [your course here] and be placed beside your fathers in peace, and have [now] perfected the work of a monk and of a pastor, the Lord wants you to endure that of a confessor, O holy shepherd.' Some of the monks saw that he seemed to be speaking with others, but they did not know the truth of the matter.

When he arrived at the *praetorium*[136] the king was told that the archbishop had come. He commanded that he be brought alone before him since he thought he would do him evil. But it happened that when he saw the saint of God and the great glory surrounding him, he was astonished, and when his eyes also saw the two apostles walking in with him, shining with light, he was in great amazement, and fear seized him. When his heart had settled down, he said gently to the archbishop, 'The stories they have told me about you: are they true?' Then [the archbishop] explained [everything] to the king with great frankness, and when he had satisfied the king he sat down beside him, as it is written, 'I will give you a spirit of wisdom which they will not be able to contradict',[a] and again, 'If they lead you before the kings and governors for my sake, do not be anxious about what you will say, for at that time the Holy Spirit will teach you the things you will say'.[β]

Then the king asked the archbishop, saying, 'I adjure you by God and by the glory which surrounds you, do not hide from me anything of what I will ask you.' The saint replied, 'I will hide nothing from you of what I know.' The king said to him, 'Who were those who were walking with you when you came in to me? I saw two men walking with you, and there was a great light surrounding you and them, the like of which I have never seen. If they had not disappeared, I would have died of fright straightaway.' Then the holy archbishop said to the king, 'These two men you saw were disciples of Christ, the King of kings, he by whom kings are kings. Moreover, those whom you saw always walk with me. That is why, O king, you should take care how [you treat] the Church. Do not afflict it! For truly, he who afflicts the Church afflicts God!' And when the king had heard these things from the archbishop, he was in great fear.

After these things, the king commanded the holy archbishop to build a church in the town of Halban[137] which he had built, and when he had completed the church in all beauty, the archbishop fell ill and was in great pain. The king was told and was saddened, and let him leave. They

---

a Cf. Lk 21:15
β Lk 12:11-12

put him [on a boat]¹³⁸ and took him to Alexandria where he worshipped in the sanctuary of Saint Mark. He was [then] ill and in pain, and when his spiritual brethren in the monastery of Scetis heard of it, they came to him and served him until the Lord visited him. So it happened that when the holy and honored archbishop was about to die, multitudes of holy saints were seated beside him, bishops, clerics, and monks, and in this way the faithful archbishop and confessor gave his spirit into the hands of God on the ninth day of Athōr.¹³⁹ He who was worthy to place his hands on his eyes was abba John, the bishop of Terenouti,¹⁴⁰ his spiritual brother, the like of Joseph who laid his hands on the eyes of his father Jacob.[a]

When they had prepared him for burial with glory and honor, the bishops and all the clerics spent the whole night singing psalms around him, and when it was morning a great crowd assembled. They celebrated the holy liturgy over him, and all the people partook of the body and the blood of the Lord. After that they laid his body by [that of] his companion,¹⁴¹ the patriarch abba John,¹⁴² in the sanctuary of Saint Mark.

His body is near us on earth, and his spirit is near God in the heavens interceding for us. And we believe that all the saints will come forth before him, the patriarchs and the
prophets, the apostles and all the saints, and we shall all
come to obtain mercy through his holy prayers
in Jesus Christ our Lord, to whom belongs
the glory with his good Father and
the Holy Spirit unto the
ages of all ages.
Amen.

---

a   Gen 50:1

NOTES

(For a List of Abbreviations the reader is referred to pages v-vi.)

1. On Coptic Pshati = Greek Nikiou and Prosōpitēs = Arabic Niqyūs, see A, nn. 99-100.

2. Amélineau, *Géographie*, 352, follows Champollion and Quatremère in identifying Pisho with the town of El-Ramleh or Ramleh-Benhā in the southern Delta, about fifty kilometers north of Cairo. The *Synaxarium*, however, says that Isaac was 'from a Borlos family' (*SAJ* [191]; O'Leary's reading of Bourgos in *SE*, 158, is simply a misprint) and Borlos (the ancient Greek Paralia) was situated on Lake Burullus in the far north of the Delta, very close to the Mediterranean coast, and just about midway between Damietta and Rosetta: see S. Timm, *Das christlich-koptische Ägypten in arabischer Zeit* (Wiesbaden, 1984-) 1:450-455, and Amélineau, *Géographie*, 104-105 (cf. Calderini, *Dizionario* [see A, n.99 above] IV/i: 52). The two statements need not necessarily be contradictory: Isaac's family may well have come from Borlos, for the *Synaxarium* does not say that he was born there. The reference in *HP* (277) to 'abba Isaac, the monk, from a Shubrā family', is, as Porcher indicates (*Vie* [6], n.1), a consequence of confusing Isaac the patriarch with Isaac the secretary (see *HP* [266] and n. 60 below).

3. This is essentially correct: Isaac/Yitsḥāq is derived from the Hebrew root *tsaḥaq* (Arabic *ḍaḥika*), which means 'to laugh'.

4. See O. H. E. KHS–Burmester, 'The Baptismal Rite of the Coptic Church', *Bulletin de la Société d'Archéologie Copte* 11 (1945) 27-86. The baptism of Isaac was, like all Coptic baptisms, by total immersion, not by affusion.

5. Lit. 'the value of the letters and also *nimathēma* (i.e. the teachings, the things learned)'. The *Synaxarium* renders the last term by 'spiritual knowledge' (*SAJ* [191]).

6. *Chaltōlarios* (Bo/Gr) = *chartularius* (Lat). In later Latin this term tended to be restricted to those who kept the records of court proceedings, but by Mēna's time the range of meanings was much wider. As we shall see below, Athanasius and Isaac, the two chamberlains of 'Abd al-'Azīz are regularly referred to as *chartularii*. Under the early muslim governors of Egypt the older roman/byzantine titles still tended to be retained (we noted the fact in our Introduction), but despite the increased knowledge we now have of this period of muslim

administration (see *ACE*, lxxvi-lxxxiii), the precise role of many of these functionaries is not always clear.

7. The term is *eparchos* (Gr), which was regularly used as the Greek equivalent of the Latin *praefectus* (see Mason, *Greek Terms* 45, 138-140, and the important discussion in C. Vandersleyen, *Chronologie des préfets d'Égypte de 284 à 395*, Collection Latomus 55 [Brussels, 1962] Chapter 13), and George is the *praefectus Aegypti/ eparchos Aigyptou* (see also nn. 11 and 133 below). Amélineau's argument, that the use of such titles indicates that we must be dealing with the period before the Arab conquest (see Amélineau, *Histoire*, xi-xiii), fails to take into account the anachronistic retention of these hellenistic forms in the early muslim period.

8. *Notarios* (Gr) = *notarius* (Lat): a stenographer, clerk, secretary, amanuensis. See Mason, *Greek Terms*, 69-70, and C. Daremberg and E. Saglio (eds.), *Dictionnaire des antiquités* (Paris, 1907; rpt. Graz, 1969) IV/i: 105-106.

9. *Synaxis* (Gr): see *ODCC*, 1314. I have translated the term by 'worship'· throughout.

10. Lit. 'underneath'.

11. *Archōn* (Gr): see Mason, *Greek Terms*, 110-113. The title is most frequently the Greek equivalent of the Latin *magistratus* 'magistrate', but as Mason observes, it could be applied to a considerable number of administrative positions. Since it is George who is summoning Menesōn in this passage, the term is here equivalent to prefect or eparch.

12. *Pretōrion* (Bo) = *praitōrion* (Gr) = *praetorium* (Lat): see Mason, *Greek Terms*, 78. The term here designates the residence of the provincial governor, George the eparch, in Alexandria. See also nn. 77 and 136 below.

13. Porcher (*Vie* [11], n. 3) suggests, reasonably, that Jacob is an error for Isaac. Isaac had only two sons; Jacob had twelve.

14. This is a very obscure addition. Porcher (*Vie* [13], n.2) suggests that it might mean 'which can be punished only to the extent that they deserve punishment', and Amélineau (*Histoire,* 8) renders it by 'things which are unattainable in the violent desire one has for them' (which is not what the Coptic text says: *ǧimpšiš* [Bo] means retribution or vengeance [see Crum, *Dictionary,* 207b], and not 'violent desire'). It might possibly mean 'things which cannot be attained because of the retribution which they will bring', but I am really not at all sure of what Mēna is saying here.

15. Coptic meditation (*meletān* [Bo/Gr]) normally refers to 'audible repetition of passages of scripture learned by heart' (see *The Life of*

Shenoute, 106, n. 67). We could therefore also translate the passage as 'These are [the texts] which the righteous [man] recites day after day'. See further H. Bacht, *Das Vermächtnis des Ursprungs,* Studien zum frühen Mönchtum I (Würzburg, 1972) 244-264: ' "Meditatio" in den ältesten Mönchquellen'. See also nn. 35 and 102 below.

16. The text actually reads 'George the secretary (*notarius*)', but this is obviously an error.

17. Scetis or Shiēt (Bo) is the Wādī'n-Naṭrūn, the centre of organized egyptian monasticism. If Isaac's parents were at Pisho (see n. 2 above), Scetis lay about seventy kilometers west, about half the distance being desert. The wādī is not, by definition, a mountain, and the common term 'mountain of Scetis' would seem to be the result of confusion between Scetis and the 'mountain of Nitria', lying some seventy-five kilometers to the north-west: for details, see Meinardus, *Christian Egypt: Ancient and Modern,* 203-206. Until very recently access to the monasteries was difficult, but since the completion of the Cairo–Alexandria desert road, there are no problems at all. The road runs within a few kilometers of the wādī, and even the tracks to the monasteries themselves have been widened and paved. This—obviously —is a mixed blessing.

18. Zacharias, *hēgoumenos* of the monastery of Saint Macarius and later bishop of Ṣā, was a disciple of the more famous John, his predecessor as *hēgoumenos* of the same monastery (see *SE,* 172; *SAJ* [465]: John is commemorated in the *Synaxarium* on 30 Choiahk [=8 January in the Gregorian calendar]). He was consecrated bishop during the patriarchate of John of Sammanūd, but apart from the information provided here by Mēna, little is known about him. Cf. *SAJ* (191), (465); *HP* (273); *SE,* 283.

19. *Hēgoumenos* (Bo/Gr): in western terms, the abbot (see *ODCC,* 618).

20. The monastery of Saint Macarius was (and is) the most important of the four monasteries of the Wādī'n-Naṭrūn: see Meinardus, *Christian Egypt: Ancient and Modern,* 209-214 (with further brief bibliography on p. 225).

21. Saïs (Gr)/Sai (Bo) is the modern Ṣā al-Ḥagar. It is situated in the western Delta on the Rosetta branch of the Nile and is about sixty-five kilometers from the coast. In its day it was a most important centre —the capital both of the Fifth Nome of Lower Egypt and of the kings of the Twenty-Sixth Dynasty, and the centre of the worship of the goddess Neith—but nothing now remains of its former glory. Earlier travellers to the site reported the traces of a huge temple enclosure, but when I visited the area in 1985, the only thing visible was a huge

pool of fetid water. See further Amélineau, *Géographie*, 405-407, and
n. 59 below.

22. Lit. 'saw revelations'.

23. In hagiographical biographies of this nature, the Coptic word
oujai would normally be translated 'salvation' (in the theological
sense). Here, however, the physical well-being of Isaac also seems to be
at stake (his parents are hunting for him with great determination),
and 'safety' may well be what is intended.

24. As we noted in the Introduction (p. 25), Terenouti is the modern
Kōm Abū Billō, lying just on the border of the desert and the Delta,
about fifty kilometers west and a little north of the monastery. It was
the main supply-base for the monasteries and the main trading-centre
for the baskets and mats which the monks produced. There was therefore constant communication between the two places. See further
the full account in Meinardus, *Christian Egypt: Ancient and Modern*,
253-263.

25. Lit. 'grass'.

26. I.e. Cyrus the Muqawqas, whom we discussed in our Introduction. As we also observed there (see A, nn. 94-96), the obvious impli-
cation of this passage is that the persecution of Cyrus is now over and
that these events must therefore be taking place after the Muslim
liberation.

27. Lit. 'manger (*ouonhf* [Bo])'.

28. There can be little doubt that the archbishop was Benjamin: see
the discussion in the Introduction, pp. 25.

29. Lit. 'fearing that they would inform the *exousia*'. As Mason
points out (*Greek Terms*, 44, 132-134), *exousia* (Gr) may have a number of meanings, but all of the most important relate to the non-
ecclesiastical administration. If it were here being used as a synonym
for magistrate (*magistratus/archōn*) (see *ibid.*, 132-133), then the
phrase could also be translated 'fearing that they would inform the
prefect'. Whatever the translation, Mēna certainly provides us with evidence that parents had a certain control over the activities of their
offspring, and that if they did not agree with the latter's choice of a
monastic vocation, they could refer the matter to the civil administration (cf. Amélineau, *Histoire*, xxi-xxii). The passage also implies that
archbishop Benjamin did not want any trouble with the government,
and if he had only recently been restored to his position thanks to
the good offices of 'Amr ibn al-'Āṣ (see pp. 17-18 of the Introduction
and A, n. 96), this is perfectly understandable.

30. Joseph's farm at Terenouti must therefore have been on the east
of the Rosetta branch of the Nile.

31. Amélineau, *Géographie*, 297-298, identifies 'the mountain of Pamaho' with the village of Bamhā/Bimhā near Gīza (more than fifty kilometers up the Nile) 'at a place where the mountain chains come very close to the river' (*ibid.*).

32. Lit. 'until the Lord persuades the heart of his parents'. The expression *thōt mphēt* (Bo: see Crum, *Dictionary*, 438) means to content or satisfy or gain agreement. See also n. 129 above.

33. Lit. 'So when they had been many days on that mountain, up to six months'.

34. Lit. 'eat his heart (*ouōm nhthēf*)': this is a standard expression in Coptic for 'repent' or, as here, 'change one's mind' (see Crum, *Dictionary*, 478b-479a). Porcher's text actually reads *ouōn nhthēf* 'open his heart', but the incorrect *ouōn* is amended to *ouōm* in his 'Les dates du patriarcat d'Isaac' (see A, n. 81 above), 221. Amélineau, *Histoire*, 15, correctly reads *ouōm*.

35. See n. 15 above: the passage could also be translated 'and walked off with each other, reciting the words of God'.

36. *Notarios/notarius*: see n. 8 above.

37. Porcher (*Vie* [23], n.1) suggests that there is a lacuna in the manuscript here. Amélineau (*Histoire,* 18) translates 'he spoke to his parents, made them give their word, and then revealed the matter to them', but he adds the note (*ibid.,* 18, n. 3): 'The turn of phrase I have used is required by the tangle of the pronouns'.

38. Lit. 'they were in a voice of joy and gladness'.

39. Lit. 'a month of days': this is the standard expression in Coptic for a month.

40. Lit. 'no *sinousia nhōout* came forth from him'. *Sinousia* (Bo)/ *synousia* (Gr) means literally 'being together', and apart from its theological meaning (it can be used to indicate the community of being shared by the three persons of the Trinity) it is frequently used in both classical and patristic Greek as an expression for sexual intercourse. *Hōout* (Bo) simply means 'male', and the whole phrase is probably meant to imply not merely the celibacy of Isaac (for there would be nothing astonishing about that), but that he never experienced ejaculation at any time, whether asleep or awake.

41. The Theologian is Gregory of Nazianzus and his views on the nature and practice of the christian life may be found conveniently summarised in D. F. Winslow, *The Dynamics of Salvation: A Study in Gregory of Nazianzus,* Patristic Monograph Series 7 (Cambridge, Mass., 1979) Chapter 7. To my great irritation, I have not yet succeeded in tracking down this precise quotation.

42. *Polētia* (Bo)/*Politeia* (Gr) means literally what one does, or how

one acts, in a city (*polis*), but by extension it came to be used not only for citizens of a *polis,* but also for citizens of a monastery. In literature of this nature it therefore means the disciplined and ascetic way of life proper to a member of a monastic community. See further *The Life of Shenoute,* 94, n. 6.

43. Lit. 'walking in a rule and a protection'. See A. Veilleux (tr.), *Pachomian Koinonia, II: Pachomian Chronicles and Rules* CS 46 (Kalamazoo, 1981) especially pp. 141ff.

44. I.e. his natural brothers. It will be remembered that Isaac came from a very wealthy Coptic family.

45. Lit. 'in the place (*topos* [Gr])'.

46. If this is a biblical quotation, I cannot trace it. Nor, apparently, could Amélineau or Porcher. There are a number of passages from which it might be derived (cf. Lk 12:47), but I have not yet found the actual words.

47. Lit. 'unblessed (*atsmou* [Sa, Bo])'. Crum, *Dictionary,* 336a, suggests that in this particular place 'the heresy of the *atsmou*' may mean 'those not taking communion', i.e. the excommunicated.

48. Amélineau suggests that Iannē (see also n. 140 below) was a Chalcedonian (see *Histoire,* xxvii-xxviii), but it is perhaps more likely that the group to which Mēna is referring are the *acephali* or *akephaloi* (see also n. 125 below), who date from the patriarchate of Peter Mongus, who followed Dioscorus's successor, Timothy the Weasel. This is the period in which the emperor Zeno was enthusiastically attempting to gain general acceptance for the *Henoticon* (see pp. 7-8 above), by which he intended to reconcile the monophysite and dyophysite factions. Peter had actually assisted Acacius, the pro-monophysite patriarch of Constantinople, in the composition of the document, and its promulgation did indeed restore some degree of harmony to the stormy relationship of Constantinople and Alexandria. Such harmony, however, was not to last. There were strong elements in Egypt (particularly among the egyptian monks) not prepared to accept anything less than a straightforward and unequivocal condemnation of the iniquitous Council of Chalcedon, and Peter had neither the authority to impose the *Henoticon* upon them nor the charisma to end their incessant complaining. And so, as Zacharias the Rhetor tells us (*Historia Ecclesiastica,* ed./tr. E. W. Brooks, CSCO Scriptores Syri III,5-6 [Paris, 1919-24] VI, 2), Peter was forced into the illogicality of accepting the *Henoticon* with one hand, and, at the same time, rejecting and condemning Chalcedon and the *Tome of Leo* with the other. This satisfied some of the monks, but certainly not all, and it was these hard-liners, totally and utterly opposed to Chalcedon,

who became the *acephali.* As their name suggests—*acephali* means 'headless ones'—they acknowledged no leader or patriarch, and would not associate with any person or party who was not prepared to condemn the Council of Chalcedon and the *Tome of Leo* unequivocally, explicitly, publicly, and totally. They also called themselves the *aposchistai,* or 'separatists', and with large and continuing support in the monasteries, harassed the monophysite patriarchs of Alexandria for decades. They certainly recognized the legitimacy of Dioscorus and they certainly refused to ally themselves with Peter. Their attitude to Timothy the Weasel is not entirely clear. See further the useful note in Sellers, *The Council of Chalcedon* (see A, n.7 above) 278-279, n. 3.

49. I.e. restored him to communion with the monophysite Church.

50. This is literally what the text says, but I suspect that the term may be a euphemism for constipated. A *ma nhemsi* 'sitting place' is certainly a standard term for a privy or latrine (see n. 51 below), and given the task which Isaac was commanded to perform in order to gain relief from his affliction, chronic constipation seems a reasonable suggestion.

51. *Nimanhemsi* (Bo): 'sitting places'. See Crum, *Dictionary,* 680b *s.v. ma nhmoos* (Sa).

52. Lit. 'word'.

53. Lit. 'God favored him with many healings'.

54. 'And had become like them' is here accidentally repeated by homoioteleuton.

55. The archbishop at this time was John of Sammanūd, the fortieth patriarch: see HP (273).

56. Lit. '*syggellos* and *notarios*'. At an earlier period a *syncellus* was much like a domestic chaplain who lived with a bishop as his confidant and adviser, but by the time of John of Sammanūd a *syncellus* was a sort of counsellor and private secretary whom a bishop or patriarch chose to live with him, assist him in his administrative work, and eventually succeed him in his office. This indeed is what happened in the case of Isaac, though his election was not uncontested. For *notarios,* see n. 8 above. See further ODCC, 1314.

57. Porcher amends the obscure word *sōif* (cf. Crum, *Dictionary,* 378b, 'meaning unknown') to the well-known *soj* (Bo) 'a fool, a madman' (see *Vie* [34], n. 2). The events referred to here are narrated in 1 Samuel 21:10-15.

58. *Ortastikē* (Bo)/*heortastikē* (Gr): the reference is to the festal letters which were circulated annually by the patriarch of Alexandria announcing the date of Easter. They could also contain considerable pastoral and exhortatory material. See, for example, Eusebius, VII,

20-23, tr. G. A. Williamson, *The History of the Church From Christ to Constantine* (Penguin Books, 1965) 302-307. See also *ODCC,* 1020-1021.

59. See nn. 18 and 21 above.

60. We are here moving in the most exalted circles. Isaac of Shubrā-tanī (see n. 61 below) was one of the two high-ranking civil servants who attended to the day-to-day administration of Egypt for the muslim governor ʿAbd al-ʿAzīz (see pp. 22 of the Introduction). The other was Athanasius, and Severus describes them thus:

> There were appointed for Abd al-Azīz two secretaries, trustworthy and orthodox, whom he set over the whole of the land of Egypt and Maryūṭ and Marākiyah and Pentapolis which is Libya. One of them was named Athanasius, and he had three sons, and was a native of Edessa in the land of Syria; while the other's name was Isaac, and he and his two sons were natives of Shubrā Tani, of a good and orthodox family (*HP* [266]).

Severus's description of Isaac and Athanasius as 'orthodox' (*urṯūduksī*) would seem to indicate that they were monophysite christians, but this is contradicted by Abū Ṣāliḥ who says specifically that the two 'christian chamberlains (*farrāshīn*)' of ʿAbd al-ʿAzīz were Melkites (Abū Ṣālih, *Churches and Monasteries of Egypt* [see A, n. 73 above] 157 [p. 67 of the Arabic text]). If this were so, it would certainly explain the antagonism which, as we shall see later, Athanasius showed towards Isaac the patriarch. The term 'secretary' (*chaltōlarios* [see n. 6 above] in Mēna's text; *kātib* in that of Severus) is not, of course, to be understood as a simple note-taker: from the story which follows here it seems that Isaac, in modern terms, might have been the Deputy Minister of Finance. See further Rizzitano, ' ʿAbd al-ʿAzīz B. Marwān' (see A, n. 65 above) 326-327.

61. Jebronathēni, as Severus indicates (see n. 60 above), is the village of Shubrā-tanī. It lies in the Delta, just about seven or eight kilometers north of Saïs (Ṣā al-Ḥagar: see n. 21 above), where Zacharias was bishop. See Amélineau, *Géographie,* 149-150.

62. *Dēmosion* (Bo/Gr): the word can mean public buildings, public affairs, or, as here, public funds or taxes. The rich revenues collected in Egypt played a major role in the economy of the Umayyad caliphate, and egyptian governors were continually under pressure to collect more and more. Egypt, for some, was simply a cow to be milked dry. See further *ACE,* 447-464; Lane-Poole, *History of Egypt in the Middle Ages,* 19-26. For the actual methods of tax-collection, one must refer to the more recent studies noted by Fraser in *ACE,* lxxxii-lxxxiii.

63. *Theōrin* (Bo)/*theōrein* (Gr): the verb may be translated as 'to contemplate', or simply as 'to see, perceive'.

64. *Solsel* (Bo): the word also means a comfort or a consolation.

65. Lit. 'the days of the Holy Forty': the phrase occurs elsewhere.

66. Abraham and George were two well-known ascetics. After the death of his father, Abraham, at the age of about thirty-five, retired to the monastery of Saint Macarius at Scetis (see nn. 17 and 20 above) where he became one of the disciples of John the Hēgoumenon (see n. 18 above). On one occasion, when he had business at 'the mountain of Aryūn (*SAJ* [533], but although *SAJ* [1036] preserves what is obviously the better reading—' [Dir] ar-Rūm—the precise location of the monastery remains unknown: see Timm, *Das christlich-koptische Ägypten* 2:791, and Amélineau, *Géographie* 59), he met George quite by chance, but such a great friendship was established between them that George left his own monastery and moved to that of Saint Macarius. Here the two friends shared the same cell until George's death in the late seventh century. See further *SAJ* (531)-(533), (1035)-(1037), and *SE* 63-64, 147. There is an Arabic translation of a *Life* of Abraham by Zacharias of Sakhā: see *GCAL* 1:472-473.

67. Lit. 'soft bread'. The bread normally available in the monasteries at this time was similar to what we would call hard tack or ship's biscuit, and it needed to be soaked before one could eat it. It was baked in quantity once or twice a year and then kept in the bread-store for distribution as necessary (see further *The Life of Shenoute,* 100, n. 34). 'Soft' or 'fresh' bread was therefore a rare luxury.

68. *Anagnōstēs* (Bo/Gr) = *lector* (Lat). A reader was one of the Minor Orders, and in the early Church his main task was the reading of the Old Testament lesson, the epistle, and, in a few places, the Gospel. For further details, see *ODCC,* 794 *s.v. lector,* and the important material in Lampe, *Lexicon,* 99-100 *s.v. anagnōstēs.* The rite of ordination of a Reader (in the modern coptic church) may be found in KHS-Burmester, *The Egyptian or Coptic Church,* 155-157. Oriōn presumably succeeded Zacharias as bishop of Saïs, but apart from the episode narrated here, I have been able to discover nothing else about him.

69. I.e. Holy Week in the west; the 'Great Week' (*al-jum'a al-kabīra*) in Egypt.

70. Lit. 'And the saint took a stupor of sleep'.

71. *Aferjōb nouōini* (Bo) means literally 'he had weakness of light', and Crum, *Dictionary,* 805b, renders it (as I have done here) 'he had weak sight'. In the present context, however, it seems to mean more than that, for the story certainly implies that the disciple was completely blind.

72. John of Sammanūd, the fortieth patriarch, whom we met earlier (see n. 55 above). For further information on John, see A, n. 64.

73. Cf. *HP* (272):

> God, the only worker of miracles, vouchsafed to the Father Patriarch acceptance and favour with the Amir, who commanded throughout the city that none should address the patriarch except with good words nor say any evil of him, and that none should hinder him in what he desired, nor in going out of the city nor coming into it.

74. On 'Abd al-'Azīz, see the account in the Introduction, pp. 20-21.

75. *Alamēr* (Bo) = *al-amīr* (Arabic): the emir, ruler, commander, or governor.

76. For Athanasius and Isaac, see n. 60 above.

77. See n. 12 above.

78. Cf. *HP* (279):

> Then ['Abd al-'Azīz] commanded to destroy all the crosses which were in the land of Egypt, even the crosses of gold and silver. So the Christians in the land of Egypt were troubled. Moreover he wrote certain inscriptions, and placed them on the doors of the churches of Miṣr and in the Delta, saying in them: 'Muḥammad is the great Apostle of God, and Jesus also is the Apostle of God. But verily God is not begotten and does not beget' (cf. Qur'ān, sūra 112).

Severus's account, however, seems to be misplaced chronologically.

79. Lit. 'Guard yourself [in your dealings] with the archbishop'.

80. According to Severus, *HP* (274), John died from a disease in his feet, arising from the gout (*niqris*). If indeed it was gout, then the uric acid might have formed calculi which would eventually block the kidneys. This would lead to a protracted and very painful death by renal failure.

81. John had actually restored and re-built the church of Saint Mark, not built it, although the arabic verbs used by Severus (*banā, 'amara*) can mean either: 'Then the magistrates and believing scribes and all the orthodox people . . . assisted [John] in the [re-]building of the church of the glorious martyr and evangelist Saint Mark; and he completed it in three years with every kind of decoration, and bought for it house-property in Miṣr and in Maryūṭ and in Alexandria. And he built a mill to grind wheat into flour for making biscuit, and a press for linseed oil, and many houses which he settled upon the church of the holy Saint Mark' (*HP* [272]).

82. According to Severus, *HP* (276), George came from Sakhā, just

about three kilometers south of the large town of Kafr al-Shaykh in the central Delta (see further Amélineau, *Géographie*, 410).

83. According to Severus, *HP* (276), the presiding bishop was Gregory of Kaïs (see n. 97 below), assisted by James of Arwāṭ, John of Nikiou (see A, n. 102), and other bishops.

84. Cf. O. H. E. KHS-Burmester, *The Rite of Consecration of the Patriarch of Alexandria* (Cairo, 1960) 9-10 (Coptic), 55 (English): 'They shall consecrate him on a Sunday, [and] when they have elected him, let them put fetters on him, and bear him to the Angelion Church (see n. 117 below) very early'; *idem, The Egyptian or Coptic Church,* 177: 'His consecration shall take place on a Sunday'. The manuscript from which the rite is translated dates from the fourteenth century, but the date of the rite itself is very much earlier (see *Rite of Consecration,* 1-3; *Egyptian . . . Church,* 174-175).

85. According to Severus, *HP* (277), the archdeacon's name was Mark.

86. Porcher, *Vie* (52), translates this phrase as 'the others, who were their subordinates', and Amélineau, *Histoire,* 45, as 'the others who had preceded them'. My own version, 'the others who happened to be there', reflects Crum, *Dictionary,* 306b *s.v. raouō* (Sa).

87. I.e. the emir, ʿAbd al-ʿAzīz. Cf. *HP* (277).

88. Babylōn (Bo) (Arabic Bābalyūn) refers not to Babylon in Asia, but to Babylon in Egypt: i.e. to Fusṭāṭ, the old muslim centre of administration and government (see A, n. 72). The name may be a corruption of old Egyptian Pi-Hapi-n-On which the Greeks then transformed into 'Babylon' by a natural process of assimilation. It was the name of the ancient fortress on the Nile, later called Qaṣr al-Shamʿa, which is now generally referred to as Old Cairo. Fusṭāṭ (also called Miṣr), the new capital founded by ʿAmr, was built adjoining the old fortress, and although the distinction between Babylon (for the fort) and Fusṭāṭ (for the town) was maintained for some time, it had begun to fade away by the beginning of the eighth century. The Arabs preferred the name Fusṭāṭ, and the Copts preferred Babylon, but among the latter the appellation was sometimes extended, 'for the Copts occasionally used Babylon to describe the whole of the great series of towns from Ḳaṣr al-Shamʿa through Fusṭāṭ and Cairo to Maṭariyye–Heliopolis. This usage then spread to western writers' (*Encyclopaedia of Islām* 1:844-845, with further bibliography, from which is unaccountably omitted the important study by A. J. Butler, *Babylon of Egypt: A Study in the History of Old Cairo* [Oxford, 1914; reprinted in *ACE*]). Part of the old fortifications are still visible and a considerable amount of restoration work is at present being carried out. It is a

wholly fascinating place to visit.

89. Cf. KHS-Burmester, *Rite of Consecration* 9 (Coptic), 54 (English):
'And the clergy and the people together shall testify on behalf of him
(and) make his election according to the canons; he being an ecclesiastic
and an unwavering virgin'. The final phrase could also be translated
'and a blameless celibate'. Cf. also *idem, Egyptian or Coptic Church,*
177: 'He must likewise be a cleric, celibate, and of middle age'. The
account of these proceedings in Severus is a little different: when the
messengers of 'Abd al-'Azīz had enquired into the matter 'they found
that the documents bore witness that it was not George of whom Abba
John [of Sammanūd] had spoken during his lifetime. So the Amir
Abd al-Azīz was angry, and cancelled George's nomination, and commanded them to appoint Isaac' (*HP* [277]).

90. The church of Saint Sergius lies almost in the middle of Babylon/
Qaṣr al-Shamʻa and is one of the oldest churches in Old Cairo. It was
built over a crypt in which, according to coptic tradition, the Holy
Family spent a month after their flight into Egypt. This crypt, which
measures about twenty feet by fifteen feet, is flooded each year during
the inundation of the Nile and is now in a somewhat precarious condition (it is closed to visitors at the moment, although, as so often in
Egypt, a suitable donation for the building and its restoration can open
many doors). The church itself is not large and if, as Mēna tells us, it
contained the people of Babylon, Alexandria, and the whole country,
they must have been somewhat constricted. When Butler visited
the church in the late nineteenth century it was a 'dim neglected
building', but this is no longer the case. Restoration work is proceeding
steadily, if slowly, and we may expect that in due course the church of
Saint Sergius will show forth once again its former splendor. See
further A. J. Butler, *The Ancient Coptic Churches of Egypt* (Oxford,
1884; rpt. 1970) 1:181-205; Meinardus, *Christian Egypt: Ancient and
Modern,* 275-279 (with a photograph of the interior among the Plates).
It should be noted that it was the election, not the consecration of Isaac
which took place in this church: his consecration took place in Alexandria, possibly in the church of the Angelion (see n. 84 above), or, if
that were too dilapidated (see n. 117 below), perhaps in the Cathedral
of Saint Mark which had been restored by John of Sammanūd (see
n. 81 above). In later times, from the election of Shenoute I in 859 to
the twelfth century, the church of Saint Sergius was regularly used for
the election of the coptic patriarch.

91. See nn. 60 and 76 above.

92. Lit. 'made him recline in front of them'. This, of course, reflects
the old roman style of dining, not the modern practice of sitting

at table on upright chairs.

93. Lit. 'he is a feeble (or powerless or timid) man' (see Crum, *Dictionary,* 805a-b *s.v. ǧbbe*), but what 'Abd al-'Azīz implies is what is translated here.

94. Cf. n. 89 above.

95. Lit. 'in choirs'.

96. The text says that John of Pshati/Nikiou (see pp. 26-27 of the Introduction) was *apotritēs* of the bishops of Upper Egypt just as Gregory of Kaïs was *apotritēs* of those of Lower Egypt. But what is an *apotritēs?* Zotenberg, *Chronique de Jean . . . de Nikiou,* 6, n.1, suggests that the word is a corruption of the Greek *epitērētēs,* 'a watcher, guardian, observer', but Amélineau, *Histoire,* xxiv, is obviously unpersuaded by this and proposes another explanation. He points out that the term also occurs in the Coptic martyrdom of John and Simon (see Hyvernat, *Actes,* 188) and that in the arabic translation of this work the term is rendered by *bitrīq,* which is an arabic adaptation of the latin *patricius* 'patrician' (in the post-classical period, 'patrician' appears as a vague honorary title in a considerable variety of circumstances: in Ibn 'Abd al-Ḥakam, for example, it is applied in its arabic form to a commissioned officer in the byzantine army: see Ibn 'Abd al-Ḥakam, *History of the Conquest of Egypt* [see A, n. 67] 175 line 20, 176 line 3 [Arabic only]). This, says Amélineau, clearly implies 'a delegation of archiepiscopal authority' (*Histoire,* xxv). Porcher's suggestion, different again, is that we read *apotritēs* as *topotērētēs* 'a legate, delegate, representative, substitute' (see *Vie* [56], n. 2). I do not know which, if any, of these explanations is correct, but all seem to imply that the bishops of Nikiou and Kaïs were recognized as having greater authority than the other bishops, and it is quite possible that at this time the two dioceses possessed a quasi-metropolitan status. See further A, n. 102 above.

97. We have a reasonable amount of information on Gregory of Kaïs. He first appears in an ill light in the *Life of Samuel of Qalamūn:* after Samuel had been persecuted by Cyrus, captured by the Berbers, released, and returned to Qalamūn, 'it happened that apa Gregory, the bishop of the city of Kaïs, and apa Jacob, his disciple, heard of the saint's fame, as also did those from his city. He went up and came to the mountain of Kalamōn because he had a great pain which troubled him day and night, for he was cruel to the image of God [i.e. humanity] and was merciless to the poor, insatiably gathering to himself masses of money. He spent every night suffering from the pain and did not allow any of those around him to sleep. But when he met the holy apa Samuel and talked with him, he saw the grace of God which was on his

face, and at the moment he greeted the saint, the pain ceased within him and he felt the cure which had happened to him. Then the bishop had great faith in the holy apa Samuel. He spent four days in the monastery and they talked with each other about the great things of God'. The bishop then left Samuel, returned to Kaïs, and sent various rich presents to the monastery of Qalamūn (Alcock, *Life of Samuel of Kalamun* [see A, n. 35] §27 p. 25 [Coptic], 101-102 [a different english translation]). According to Severus, Gregory lived in the time of Agathon (*HP* [263]); he was present, together with John of Nikiou and other bishops, at the death of John of Sammanūd (*HP* [274]); he was involved in the attempt to elect George of Sakhā in place of Isaac (see n. 83 above); under Isaac's successor, Simon, he supervised the building of two churches at Ḥalwān (see *HP* [296] and Abū Ṣāliḥ, *Churches and Monasteries of Egypt,* 155-156); and in the three year period between the death of Simon and the election of his successor Alexander he was sent to Alexandria by ʿAbd al-ʿAzīz, apparently with patriarchal authority, to administer the church in the interregnum (*HP* [303]). In other words, if all these references are to one and the same Gregory (and they appear to be), he was bishop from the patriarchate of Agathon (who was consecrated in about 665: see A, n. 62) to that of Alexander, who was consecrated in about 704. His meeting with Samuel of Qalamūn may also be fitted into this period since Samuel did not die until the last years of the seventh century (cf. Alcock, *Life of Samuel,* ix). In Butler's account (*ACE,* 185-186, n. 2) the dates require some amendment, and the episcopate of Gregory might have covered not a period of upwards of fifty years (which would, admittedly, be unusual), but a period of upwards of thirty-five, which would not be especially uncommon. We have no need, therefore, of positing two Gregories of Kaïs. The town of Kaïs itself was a long way south of Alexandria, just about double the distance to Cairo, near the site of the ancient Oxyrhynchus (the modern al-Bahnasā) (see Amélineau, *Géographie,* 395-397).

98. Lit. 'came before him'.

99. I.e. Sunday, 4 December 690: for a full discussion of the dates of Isaac's patriarchate, see the relevant section of the Introduction. For the location of his consecration, see n. 90 above.

100. Lit. 'was fulfilled over him'.

101. *Hysichazin* (Bo) = *hesychazein* (Gr): 'to be quiet, tranquil, silent, recollected'. It is the verb from which the term hesychasm is derived and it was to become a word of great importance and great richness in later greek theology.

102. Or 'recite the holy scriptures': see nn. 15 and 35 above.

103. *Synaxis:* see n. 9 above.

104. The *anaphora* (Gr: 'offering') is the most important part of the Divine Liturgy. It begins with the introductory material to the *epiklēsis* (see n. 105 below) and continues to the end of the communion. See further KHS-Burmester, *Egyptian or Coptic Church,* 46-49 (with further bibliography).

105. I.e. the *epiklēsis* (Gr: 'invocation'), when the priest beseeches the Father to send down the Holy Spirit on the bread and wine and thereby change them into the body and blood of Christ: see *ibid.* 67-68, 93-94; *ODCC* 456 (with further bibliography).

106. Athanasius the Great, the twentieth patriarch, who was the great champion of the Nicene faith and the defender of the *homoousios:* see J. Quasten, *Patrology* (Utrecht/Antwerp/Westminster, 1963) 3: 20-79. For the coptic view, see the lengthy and interesting account in *HP* (139)-(159); *SAJ* (1002)-(1004).

107. Cyril of Alexandria, the twenty-fourth patriarch, whose involvement in the great christological controversy we discussed briefly in our Introduction. See further Quasten, *Patrology* 3:116-142.

108. According to Amélineau, *Géographie,* 373, Psanasho is to be identified with the small village of Shanshā, situated in the central Delta in the neighborhood of Sammanūd.

109. Lit. 'reclining': see n. 92 above.

110. See nn. 60 and 76 above. Athanasius was a Syrian from Edessa (see n. 60) and despite his initial antagonism to Isaac he was responsible for the restoration of the church of the Angelion in Alexandria (see n. 117 below) and, at an earlier date, for the foundation of two churches in Babylon: 'According to Eutychius (says Butler) the church of Māri Girgis was built about the year 684 A.D., by one Athanasius, a wealthy scribe, who also founded the church of Abu Ḳīr "within Ḳaṣr-ash-Shamm'ah" ' (Butler, *Ancient Coptic Churches* 1:249). After the death of 'Abd al-'Azīz in 704, when the egyptian Christians once again began to suffer persecution (see p. 22 of our Introduction), Athanasius went to Damascus to see 'Abd al-Malik (see A, n. 66), but was there arrested and his goods confiscated (see *HP* [308]). What happened to him after this is unknown, but Severus reports an Athanasius who died in Antioch during the patriarchate of Michael I (the forty-sixth patriarch, who was consecrated in about 743), and if this is the Athanasius we are discussing here (and so it would seem to be), he must have been a very old man at the time of his death (see *HP* [368]).

111. Lit. 'for truly the *exousia* was in his hands'. On *exousia,* see n. 29 above. That Athanasius did indeed wield the *exousia* is confirmed by

Severus who speaks of him as presiding over (*mutawallīn*) the *dīwān* (see *HP* [302]): in other words, he was acting as a sort of Prime Minister for 'Abd al-'Azīz.

112. The verb is *er-nēmphin* (Bo) and is obviously Greek. But what greek word is here represented? Porcher, *Vie* (61), n. 4, suggests we amend it to *memnēsthai* (from *mimnēskō* 'call to mind, remember') and accordingly translates the phrase as 'he remembered nothing'. Amélineau, without explanation, renders it as 'il n'avait pas son esprit' (*Histoire*, 54). I would prefer to derive it from *nēphein* 'to be sober, sane, alert' and hence translate it here as 'Athanasius was wholly distracted, or out of his mind with worry and grief', and at n. 113 below as 'when Isaac recovered from, or was restored to normality after, the revelation'. Cf. Alcock, *Life of Samuel of Kalamun*, 3 lines, 21-22.

113. *Ernēmphin:* see n. 112 above.

114. Abba Gregory is probably Gregory of Kaïs (see n. 97 above), but I've been able to find no information on George, or Piamot of Damietta.

115. For Athanasius and Cyril, see nn. 106-107 above. Ignatius is Ignatius of Antioch, bishop of the city in the late first and early second centuries. One of the Apostolic Fathers, he left an interesting collection of letters written during his journey from Antioch to Rome where, according to tradition, he was martyred in about 107 (see further *ODCC*, 676-677; *SAJ* [440]-[441]). Severus (c. 465-538) was the monophysite patriarch of Antioch and a leading opponent of the Council of Chalcedon. He was of great importance in the organization of the monophysite movement and, in his voluminous and acute theological writings, one of the most influential and persuasive proponents of the moderate monophysite position. The old study by J. Lebon, *Le Monophysisme sévérien* (Louvain, 1909) remains of fundamental importance, but there is need of a modern and comprehensive examination of this impressive theologian. See further *ODCC*, 1247; Frend, *The Rise of the Monophysite Movement* (see A, n. 10) Index *s.v.* Severus; *SE*, 249-250; *SAJ* (789)-(791). Athanasius' invocation of the two Antiochenes, Ignatius and Severus, as well as the two Alexandrians, Athanasius and Cyril, may perhaps reflect his own syrian background.

116. For *parousia* (Bo/Gr), read *parrēsia* 'familiarity, intimacy, confidence, freedom of speech, trust, openness'. See also n. 135 below.

117. The church of the Angelion or Evangelion (Butler suggests the former name may be more correct: see *ACE*, 52, n.2 and 444, n.2) was one of the most important churches in Alexandria. According to Meinardus, it was built by the thirty-third patriarch, Theodosius I (who died in 567), and was wholly destroyed in the tenth century

(see *Christian Egypt: Ancient and Modern,* 167-168). It stood in the citadel, a short distance from Pompey's (or Diocletian's) Pillar, and according to an early tradition, it was here that the alexandrian patriarchs were consecrated (see n. 84 above). See further *ACE,* 385-386; Calderini, *Dizionario* I/i:166.

118. This obviously refers to some monophysite synod located in Alexandria but I have so far been unable to find any further information about it.

119. I.e. the Melkites, not the Muslims or the Persians.

120. I.e. 'Abd al-'Azīz. Cf. n. 87 above.

121. I.e. John of Sammanūd. See nn. 55 and 72 above.

122. Lit. 'before the king'.

123. Alban (Bo) = Ḥalwān/Ḥulwān/Ḥelwān (Arabic). This is the town south of Cairo/Fusṭāṭ to which 'Abd al-'Azīz, primarily for reasons of health, moved the centre of administration. For a discussion and description, see the Introduction, p. 21.

124. Lit. 'into his house'.

125. *Niataphe* (Bo): 'the headless ones' (see Crum, *Dictionary,* 14a). For the Acephalites, see n. 48 above.

126. Amélineau, *Géographie* 284, provides no location for Nioubershenoufi and says that in his view 'this place was simply a diocese having no connection with either the Jacobite or orthodox administration'. Mohammed Ramzi Bey, however, in his corrections to Amélineau's work, notes that there was a village of this name and that it still exists today: it is Shnūfa, near the district capital of Shibīn el-Kawm in Manūfīyyah province (i.e. in the south-central Delta, one of the most fertile parts of the whole region): see M. Ramzi Bey, 'Rectifications à l'ouvrage d'É. Amélineau, *Géographie de l'Égypte à l'époque copte'*, in *Mélanges Maspero: III, Orient Islamique* (Cairo, 1940) 298 (despite its title, this article is in Arabic).

127. Lit. 'the'.

128. *Eulogia* (Bo/Gr). This is the *panis benedictus*—the *antidōron* of modern Orthodoxy—which is bread prepared for the eucharist and blessed by the priest, but not consecrated. It is distributed after the Divine Liturgy to those who, for various reasons, feel themselves unworthy or unprepared to receive the actual eucharistic elements, but yet wish to assert and to demonstrate their participation in the mystical body of the christian community. Since it is not the true Body of Christ it may therefore be distributed more widely and with much greater freedom than the actual consecrated bread and wine. See further Lampe, *Lexicon,* 570 *s.v. eulogia,* §E.

129. The verb is *thōt mphēt* which we discussed at n. 32 above.

130. I.e. Athanasius and Isaac.

131. Lit. 'the whole multitude'.

132. Severus (*HP* [278]) speaks not of Makouria and Maurōtania, but of Abyssinia and Nubia. Amélineau, however, offers a more precise identification: Makouria is the area around Dongola and Kōrti (now part of the Sudān), and Maurōtania is the country of the Blemmyes (see the *Life of Shenoute,* 105, n. 66), that part of Nubia just south of Aswān (see Amélineau, *Histoire,* xxxiii-xxxv; *idem,* 'Sur deux documents coptes' [see A, n. 110] 350-351; Abū Ṣāliḥ, *Churches and Monasteries of Egypt,* 261, nn. 2-3). It is therefore impossible to go down the Nile from the southern Sudān/Makouria to Egypt without passing through Nubia/Maurōtania.

133. Lit. 'the augustal (*augoustali* [Bo])'. From the late fourth century the prefect of Egypt (*praefectus Aegypti*) took the title of augustal prefect (*praefectus augustalis*) (the term first occurs in the Theodosian Code of 382), and the augustal is therefore the same person as the eparch who appears in n. 7 above. See Daremberg and Saglio, *Dictionnaire* (see n. 8 above) IV/i:616.

134. See n. 69 above.

135. For *parousia* read *parrēsia* as in n. 116 above.

136. See n. 12 above.

137. Halban = Alban = Ḥalwān: see n. 123 above. Cf. Abū Ṣāliḥ, *Churches and Monasteries of Egypt,* 155-156: '[There is at Ḥulwān] a monastery named after the Lady Mary, the Pure Virgin. It was erected at the expense of the bishops, in the patriarchate of Anbā Isaac the monk, who was the forty-first in the order of succession, and in the patriarchate of his successor, Anbā Simon the Syrian, the forty-second patriarch, during the governorship of 'Abd al-'Azīz ibn Marwān, through the agency of Gregory, bishop of Al-Ḳais. The monastery is called the monastery of Abū Ḳarkar; the last word being derived from the name of Gregorios'. Cf. also *HP* (278).

138. This is what the text implies, although it does not say so specifically.

139. I.e. 5 November. For a full discussion of the date of Isaac's death, see the relevant section of the Introduction.

140. For Terenouti, see n. 24 above. John of Terenouti might possibly be the Iannē whom we met earlier (see nn. 47-48 above). Mēna tells us there that in later years he became Isaac's companion and was, in due course, consecrated bishop.

141. *Šjēr* in Porcher's text (*Vie* [88]) is a typographical error for *šphēr* 'companion'.

142. John of Sammanūd: see nn. 55, 72, and 121 above.

THE MARTYRDOM OF SAINT MACROBIUS

INTRODUCTION

THE HISTORICAL BACKGROUND

COPTIC MARTYRDOMS are not to everyone's taste. They are a curious form of literature, dripping with blood and righteousness, and demanding a willing suspension of disbelief undreamed of by Samuel Taylor Coleridge.[1] They lack originality; they follow a stereotyped pattern; and to commend them they have neither the historical accuracy of the events they relate nor the oratorical eloquence of the language in which they are presented. But for all that, there is no doubt that in Egypt they enjoyed great popularity, and the *Martyrdom of Saint Macrobius* here presented is a straightforward and standard example of this unique literary genre.

The cult of the martyrs has an ancient history.[2] In the earliest church of the New Testament the term was used of the Apostles who 'witnessed' (and 'witness' is what 'martyr' means) the resurrection of Jesus of Nazareth and who were then called upon to 'witness' to this event throughout the world. 'Lord', they said, 'will you at this time restore the kingdom to Israel?' He said to them, 'It is not for you to know times or seasons which the Father has fixed by his own authority. But you shall receive power when the Holy Spirit has come upon you; and you shall be my witnesses (*martyres*) in Jerusalem and in all Judea and Samaria and to the end of the earth'.[3] But with the onset and spread of persecution in the later first century, the title became restricted to those who had not only witnessed to the faith, but had suffered in so doing; and, eventually, to those who had suffered and had died. Those who survived were called the confessors.

The methods of martyrdom were often extremely unpleasant. It is true that some of the more absurd ingenuities which we find in the later sagas have little credibility, but the historical horrors which we know to have occurred are quite sufficient to revolt our sensibilities and arouse our admiration.

> Some, suffering the punishment of parricides, were shut up in a sack with snakes and thrown into the sea; others were tied to huge stones and cast into a river. For Christians the cross itself was not deemed sufficient agony; hanging on the tree, they were beaten with rods until their bowels gushed out, while vinegar and salt were rubbed into their wounds. In the Thebais, during the persecution of Diocletian, Christians were tied to catapults, and so wrenched limb from limb. Some, like Ignatius, were thrown to the beasts; others tied to their horns. Women were stripped, enclosed in nets, and exposed to the attacks of furious bulls. Many were 'made to lie on sharp shells', and tortured with scrapers, claws, and pincers, before being delivered to the mercy of the flames. Not a few were broken on the wheel, or torn in pieces by wild horses. Of some the feet were slowly burned away, cold water being poured over them the while

lest the victims should expire too rapidly. Peter, one of the servants of Diocletian, was scourged to the bone, then placed near a grid-iron that he might witness the roasting of pieces torn from his own body. At Lyons they tried to overcome the obstinacy of Sanctus of Vienne 'by fixing red-hot plates of brass to the most delicate parts of his body'. After this he was slowly roasted in the iron chair. Down the backs of others 'melted lead, hissing and bubbling, was poured'; while a few, 'by the clemency of the emperor', escaped with the searing out of their eyes, or the tearing off of their legs. These instances—but a few out of a long catalogue that might be compiled—will show what it cost to witness the good confession; to say nothing of the rack, the hobby-horse, the claws, and other tortures preparatory to the sentence.[4]

It is only to be expected, therefore, that those who experienced this sort of agony and yet had not lapsed should be highly honored by the church, and likewise, that they should be considered to have especial powers of persuasion and intercession with God.

Thus, from the end of the second century the cult of the martyrs spread rapidly, and the martyrs, their relics, and their festivals enjoyed greater and greater importance in the practice of popular Christianity. A martyr is a useful person to have around. It is always advisable to have a friend at court, and if one is perhaps a little unsure of the unsullied perfection of one's earthly life, and just a little fearful of how severely the Almighty Judge will regard one's inevitable peccadilloes, it is a comfort and a consolation to have as a friend someone who has the ear of God and may therefore say a word or two to Him on your behalf. It is true that Christ, the God-Man, was the perfect Mediator and Advocate, but whereas in the case of Christ one was certain of his divinity and believed in his humanity, in the case of the martyrs their humanity was manifestly more obvious, and it might therefore be expected that their acquaintance with sin was more intimate and their sympathies more easily aroused than was ever the case with Christ. Added to this, they were, in many cases, local, and unlike Christ, who had ascended soul and body into heaven, the martyrs had left little bits of themselves behind to act as psychic links to the Other World.

It is quite understandable, therefore, that the martyrs came to be figures of the utmost importance in popular Christianity, and in rural Egypt, where literacy was limited and the *fellahīn* uneducated, the martyr-cult took seed, germinated, blossomed, and flourished in the most fertile soil imaginable. Not all approved of it. In the fifth century, no less a force than Shenoute the Great fulminated against it, pointing to its absurdities and condemning its abuses. He was well aware that since every village demanded its own shrine, bones of any sort and vintage were being dug up and venerated as the true and authentic relics of this or that martyr. But is it only martyrs who are buried, says Shenoute? How do you know whose bones they are? They might be those of a hustler or a whore or any godless individual. They might even be those of a dog. Nor does he have any time for the visions and dreams by which the bones are supposedly 'authenticated', and the quest for healing at a 'martyr's' shrine is too close to the paganism he abhors to be in any way tolerated. The cult of the christian saint is not Shenoute's Christianity.[5]

Yet, as O'Leary says, 'these criticisms . . . did little to check the popular movement and every village erected its martyr's shrine, just as now it has the shrine of a Muslim sheikh, and in earlier times had the shrine of a pagan diety. The occupation of these sacred sites was more or less continuous: where the sick were laid before the god's shrine, there they were laid before the martyr's tomb, and there they are still placed before the sheikh's tomb'.[6] What is so tempting is the immediate access. God is a busy person—he has the universe to govern—but a local saint, be he Muslim or Christian, is, by definition, *local*. He is concerned with *your* village, *your* people, and if you have a problem with your neighbors or your garbage collection, you contact your local headman, not the President of Egypt or the appointed ruler of your nation.

The popularity of the martyr-cult in Egypt demanded a multitude of martyrs, and historical circumstances certainly provided them. The first systematic, state-sponsored persecution, occurred at the very beginning of the third century under Septimius Severus, and then, after a short respite, the emperor Decius and his successor Valerian launched a more vicious and more wide-spread wave of persecution in the decade following the year 250. But in 284 (according to coptic tradition) the emperor Diocletian ascended the throne and it was in his reign that the Christians of Egypt were subjected to the most ferocious and systematic slaughter hitherto experienced. It is he who, of all the anti-christian emperors, was the most loathed by the Copts and it is his name, above all, which appears consistently in the martyrdoms as the *bête noire* of egyptian Christianity.

In fact, Diocletian was not the bloody-minded savage so often depicted in the egyptian martyrdoms. He was a man with a real genius for organization and administration, and many of the reforms and reorganizations he implemented were to last for centuries. But he was also deeply concerned about any threat to the unity of the Roman Empire—a unity which, he considered, could best be maintained by the old roman traditions, roman values, and roman religion—and he saw the rapid rise and spread of Christianity as a major threat to imperial unity.[7] In addition to this, he listened all too carefully to the advice of Galerius, his Caesar of the East, and Galerius was a tough and uneducated soldier who, it seems, despised Christians on principle.[8] Thus, between them, Galerius and Diocletian launched the Great Persecution in 303, demanding the destruction of christian churches, the burning of christian literature, the confiscation of christian property, the removal of all christians from state offices, and the banning of christian communal worship. But, says Aziz Atiya, 'the Christians were no longer a mere handful of nonconformists':

> They were now sufficiently numerous to retaliate; and when they did, the Roman law was inflicted upon them without compassion. The result was a most formidable wave of persecution and martyrdom. The intensity of the movement varied from country to country, and Egypt appears to have fared worse than many or all. Maiming and mutilation, blinding, slow diabolical torture and burning were amongst the barbarous savageries which the imperial agents employed in the destruction of their victims. Outright decapitation was an unusual act of mercy and a privilege rarely granted . . . The number of martyrs was legion. The dungeons were full of men and women of all classes and stations in life, awaiting their turn for the rack for the gallows.[9]

The impact of this dreadful period on the egyptian Christians was so profound that in later centuries they determined to reckon the history of their church not from the traditional date of the birth of Christ, but from the accession of Diocletian on 29 August 284. This calendrical usage may be witnessed in the sixth century, though it was not adopted officially until two centuries later, and the formal designation *Anno Martyrorum* (AM), or the Era of the Martyrs, does not appear until the eleventh century.[10]

THE LITERARY FORM OF THE MARTYRDOMS

In an admirable and indispensable study first published in 1921, Hippolyte Delehaye, the *doyen* of hagiographical studies, distinguished clearly three types of martyrdom: (i) the historical passions; (ii) the panegyrics; and (iii) the epic passions.[11] In the first case we are dealing with genuine contemporary accounts of the events which took place, and these (with the usual precautions) we may accept as reasonably accurate descriptions of the sufferings and deaths of the persons involved. One example is the moving account of the martyrdom of Polycarp; another is the important passion of Perpetua and Felicity.[12] In the second case we are concerned with orations from the mouths of those who represent 'the Golden Age of christian eloquence'[13]: theologians such as the Cappadocian Fathers or John Chrysostom. Here we have moved from the era of actual persecution to the more tolerant world of Constantine and his successors, and since the christian preachers could now appear and joyfully proclaim in public the role played by the glorious dead in sustaining the Great Church through all the years of suffering and savagery, so their eulogies become ever more florid and more elaborate: panegyrics designed for public consumption, and not simple accounts intended for private circulation.[14]

And then, inevitably, the panegyric gave way to the epic passion, or, as Delehaye calls it elsewhere, the 'artificial' martyrdom.[15] Here we have left the realms of history and have entered a fictitious universe of marvel and miracle, where death has no dominion, logic is lost, and anything may happen. Here we find the fairy-tale passions of the hustlers, whores, and dogs whom Shenoute decries: passions to suit every sort of martyr, whether they ever existed or not, and passions which, with few exceptions, follow a standard and stereotyped pattern which we shall discuss in due course. For this literature Father Delehaye had little time: 'The artificial character of this wretched literature is immediately evident', he wrote, 'It proceeds by commonplaces, and often by borrowings; and a detailed study will permit us only to say to what degree our hagiographers have practised plagiarism'.[16] It offends both history and common-sense, he continues, and the only thing about it which is in any way useful is the information it provides on topography. This, of course, is important, since the establishment of a historical link between a locality and a martyr is the normal means of demonstrating the existence of a cult.[17]

Despite the efforts of scholars such as Reymond and Barns to shed a somewhat more positive light on these writings,[18] much of what Delehaye said remains true. To read one is to read twenty, and the occasional poetical passage, memorable prayer, or genuine historical snippet, represents but a small oasis in a desert of preposterous fiction. If Delehaye's judgment was too severe, it was not too severe by much, and even though it is now recognized that these sagas do contain certain authentic historical echoes, they can never be considered as great literature.

The main events in the martyrdom of Macrobius will serve to illustrate the established pattern which, with minor variations, is followed throughout:

1) the saint is brought before the pagan tribunal sometime during the reign of the iniquitous Diocletian;

2) he is accused of being a Christian and is offered his freedom if he recants;

3) he refuses, frequently accompanying his refusal with what Reymond and Barns splendidly describe as 'fantastic feats of provocative rudeness'[19];

4) he is then tortured for the first time;

5) after the tortures prove ineffective, the saint is sent down the Nile to another governor (in the case of Macrobius, this governor is Armenius, a well-known character);

6) he is imprisoned and there receives visionary comfort from Christ (or, in many cases, from the archangel Michael);

7) he is then brought before the new governor, and after again refusing to recant, is tortured for the second time, again to no effect;

8) the governor now turns conciliatory and tries to persuade, rather than force, the saint to recant;

9) the latter, naturally, refuses, and is again rude to the governor;

10) as a consequence of this the governor loses all control and orders the third set of ingenious tortures which culminate, normally, in decapitation and the eventual death of the martyr. At any time in this sequence there may occur miracles or healings, and the by-standers are converted *en masse* by the saint's achievements. They, too, may then become martyrs.[20]

It is obvious that with a standard format such as this, minor changes in, for example, tribunal personnel, tortures, and miracles can produce quite different martyrdoms for quite different martyrs, but the essential similarity of the texts may be seen from the fact, pointed out by Reymond and Barns, that if a phrase or passage is missing or defective in one passion, it is often possible to emend it by its doublet in another.[21] It is clear, too, that such artificial construction essentially precludes any useful discussion of authorship. Delehaye suggests that the epic passions were produced to order in a workshop in Alexandria—'une école d'hagiographes' —and that the most important piece of their equipment would be 'that instrument dear to hagiographers of all countries': a pair of scissors.[22]

What, then, of the attribution of the Martyrdom of Saint Macrobius to Mēna of Nikiou? It is obvious that it cannot be proved, and as we have just observed, the whole structure of these epic passions prevents any useful considerations of individual authorship. One *compiles* a martyrdom; one does not create it. The task is like mounting stamps in an album: the names, colors, and arrangements may vary from page to page, but one is not expected to print one's own stamps in order to become a philatelist. Mēna might well have compiled the Martyrdom of Saint Macrobius (and the considerable stylistic differences between it and the *Life of Isaac of Alexandria* would be a natural consequence of compilation), but many other people might have done so as well.

The epic martyrdom is similar in many ways to a movie cartoon. I am thinking especially of the Road-Runner and

the Coyote, but any of the others which pit the Good and
Innocent (e.g. Tweety-Pie or Jerry) against the Bad and
Wicked (e.g. Sylvester or Tom) will serve the purpose. Here
we have light and darkness in continual contention, and each
is quite unmistakable: there are no grey areas in a cartoon.
Further, as we watch all the fiendish and ingenious plans and
devices which the Coyote invents to capture his prey, we,
the audience, can sit back and enjoy it all the more because
we know that there is no possible way that the Road-Runner
can ever be caught. Not only this, but after all the Coyote's
plans have once more gone disastrously awry and we have
seen him flattened by a steam-roller or blown to a thousand
pieces by his own gun, we are in no way surprised when, in
the next scene, he appears whole and alive and as eager as
ever to pursue his unharmed and innocent victim. And when
the cartoon is over, we can look forward to the next one,
despite the fact that the only variations which can possibly
occur lie in the Coyote's ineffectual attempts to capture his
uncapturable prey. That he will fail, as he always fails, is not
in doubt.

This is the world of the epic martyrdom. The martyr is the
superhuman hero who cannot be harmed by human means.[23]
The emperor and his governors are the Coyotes, who, with an
infinity of malice, devise the most painful punishments and
the most terrible tortures imaginable. And we are the
audience who know that (until God permits it) death will
not follow and all their plans must come to naught, that the
hero will escape as he always escapes, and that in the end
Good must triumph over Evil. To compare the martyrdom
of Macrobius with, say, the martyrdom of Polycarp is
absurd—we do not watch Sylvester or Tweety-Pie in order to
gain practical advice on how to look after cats or canaries—
but to compare it with an egyptian romance or fairy-tale may
be more reasonable.[24] In this context, the plethora of
tortures and repeated resuscitations become perfectly believ-
able, but we must listen to the stories like the little child of

Matthew 18:3 and not read them as if they were an academic biography.

On the other hand, there are such things as coyotes and road-runners, and the charming backgrounds which film animators drew in so carefully do reflect certain parts of America. Similarly, in the martyrdom of Macrobius (for example) there may well appear true, if distorted, historical information.[25] There is no sound reason to doubt the existence of the holy Macrobius, and he probably did succeed Sarapamōn as bishop of Nikiou in the early fourth century. And when we are told that he came from the village of Ǧmoumi—Ashmūn in the southern Delta, about forty kilometers north-west of Cairo[26]—this, too, may reflect a local and accurate tradition. In just the same way, we must not dismiss the information about Theophanes the *tabularius* and the report (in the Martyrdom of Macarius of Antioch) that he had built a temple to Sip somewhere in the neighborhood.[27] But as I observed above, such historical information is the exception rather than the rule, and it is sometimes as difficult to extract the facts from these artificial martyrdoms as it is to separate the gin from the vermouth in a dry martini.

The epic passions, with their multiple martyrdoms, are a particularly egyptian creation and, like much else in that remarkable country, may not be to western christian taste. Yet despite their absurdities, they remain a genuine reflection of the horrors which egyptian Christianity survived, and it is perhaps understandable that a church whose early days were soaked in so much blood would not have wished to forget such a holocaust. But for us, if we are to read and enjoy the following pages, it would be wise to take to heart the advice given by the White Queen to Alice when she, like so many others, said she could not believe impossibilities:

> 'Can't you?' the Queen said in a pitying tone. 'Try again: draw a long breath, and shut your eyes.'
> Alice laughed. 'There's no use trying,' she said,

'one *can't* believe impossible things.' 'I daresay you haven't had much practice,' said the Queen. 'When I was your age, I always did it for half-an-hour a day. Why, sometimes I've believed as many as six impossible things before breakfast.'[28]

NOTES

(For a List of Abbreviations the reader is referred to pages v-vi.)

1.   S. T. Coleridge, *Biographia Literaria* (London, 1817) Chapter 14.

2.   See, for example, W. H. C. Frend, *Martyrdom and Persecution in the Early Church* (Oxford, 1965) (a superb study), and H. Delehaye, *Les origines du culte des martyrs,* Subsidia Hagiographica xx (Brussels, 1912). There is a large literature on this subject.

3.   Acts 1:6-8 (RSV).

4.   H. B. Workman, *Persecution in the Early Church* (Oxford, 1906; rpt. 1980) 120. See further H. Delehaye, *Les passions des martyrs et les genres littéraires,* Subsidia Hagiographica xiiiB (Brussels, 1966²) 197-207. See also n. 9 below.

5.   See J. Leipoldt, *Schenute von Atripe und die Entstehung des national ägyptischen Christentums* (Leipzig, 1903) 183-184, and H. Delehaye, *Les martyrs d'Égypte* (Brussels, 1923) 36-39. Nor did Pachomius approve: see L. T. Lefort, *Les vies coptes de saint Pachôme et ses premiers successeurs,* Bibliothèque du Muséon 16 (Louvain, 1943) 49-50.

6.   *SE,* 13.

7.   For a brief, accurate and convenient account of Diocletian, see N. G. L. Hammond and H. H. Scullard, eds., *The Oxford Classical Dictionary* (Oxford, 1970²) 346-347. For the coptic view, see *SE,* 16-18.

8.   See the *Oxford Classical Dictionary,* 455.

9.   Atiya, *History of Eastern Christianity* (see A, n. 9) 31. For more detailed accounts of the Great Persecution, see the *Cambridge Ancient History,* Volume 12 (Cambridge, 1939) Chapter 19: 'The Great Persecution' (by N. H. Baynes), and Frend, *Martyrdom and Persecution,* Chapter 15 (with a comprehensive bibliography on pp. 595-598). Frend also provides the most sensible discussion of the numbers of Christians who perished: see *ibid.* 536-537.

10.   See *SE,* 34-35; Meinardus, *Christian Egypt: Ancient and Modern,* 70-71. As O'Leary says, 'To reduce a year of the "Era of the Martyrs" to Anno Domini add 283 years and 240 days' (*SE,* 34-35).

11.   See Delehaye, *Passions des martyrs, passim.*

12.   See, for example, H. Musurillo, *The Acts of the Christian Martyrs* (Oxford, 1972) 2-21 (Polycarp), 106-131 (Perpetua and Felicity) (Greek texts and English translations). Further on this type of passion,

see the excellent study by G. Lanata, *Gli atti dei martiri come documenti processuali* (Milan, 1973).

13.   Delehaye, *Passions des martyrs,* 171.

14.   See *ibid.,* 133-169.

15.   *Ibid.,* 13.

16.   Delehaye, *Martyrs d'Égypte,* 148.

17.   *Ibid.*

18.   See E. A. E. Reymond and J. W. B. Barns, *Four Martyrdoms From the Pierpont Morgan Coptic Codices* (Oxford, 1973) 1-2, 6-8 (the whole of their introduction is essential reading).

19.   *Ibid.,* 2.

20.   For a more detailed account of the stereotyped pattern of the epic martyrdom, see Delehaye, *Passions des martyrs,* 171-226.

21.   Reymond/Barns, *Four Martyrdoms,* 2.

22.   See Delehaye, *Martyrs d'Égypte,* 152.

23.   See Delehaye, *Passions des martyrs,* 172-173.

24.   Cf. Reymond/Barns, *Four Martyrdoms,* 1-2.

25.   See *ibid.,* 6-8, and Vandersleyen, *Chronologie des préfets d'Égypte* (see B, n. 7) Chapter 12.

26.   See Amélineau, *Géographie,* 182, though Amélineau has here confused Macrobius of Nikiou with Macarius of Antioch.

27.   See Hyvernat, *Actes,* 74-75: 'When the eparch Eulogios went south in Egypt and saw the splendid (lit. 'adorned') temple of Sip (Sepa?: see W. Helck and E. Otto, eds., *Lexicon für Ägyptologie* V/6 [Wiesbaden, 1984] 859-863). he asked their headman about it, saying, "What is this?" And straightaway the Christians from Ǧmouni came to him and told him how Diophanes had built the temple, and that it was he who had killed abba Makrobi [Macrobius], the bishop of their district. When he had heard these things, Eulogios commanded [them] to bring up the bones of the impious Diophanes from the place in which they were buried, and had them burned in a fire in accordance with the prophecy of the holy bishop abba Makrobi. And he also burned the temple, razed it to its foundations, and killed every pagan he found'.

28.   Lewis Carroll, *Alice Through the Looking Glass,* Chapter 5.

THE MARTYRDOM OF SAINT MACROBIUS

A EULOGY DELIVERED BY ABBA MĒNA, THE
MOST PIOUS BISHOP OF THE CHRIST-LOVING
CITY OF PSHATI,[1] FOR OUR MOST HOLY
AND THRICE-BLESSED FATHER, THE HOLY
ABBA MACROBIUS, THE BISHOP AND THE
MARTYR, OF THIS SAME CITY OF PSHATI,
ON THE DAY OF HIS ILLUSTRIOUS COMEM-
MORATION, THE SECOND OF THE MONTH
PHAMENŌTH.[2] IN THE PEACE OF GOD. AMEN.[3]

IN SEEING NOW, O pious people, your zeal and your
abundant love for the great abba Macrobius,[4] at once
virgin, bishop, and martyr, my heart rejoices and encour-
ages my feeble understanding to pronounce his eulogy. But
forgive me, O Christ-loving people, if, as I go towards this
great sea—for such is the commemoration of that great
[saint]—I should be a little overcome in the discourse, for I
am unlearned in these sorts of exercise. Yet when I see your
zeal and your assembly, I feel as if I have almost forgotten
my own weakness. Being seized by your zeal, you have
strengthened my heart and encouraged my sluggish understanding to speak of the memory of the martyr of Christ, the
great abba Macrobius, for whom indeed we are gathered here
today. For 'the memory of the righteous is a good report',[a]
as Solomon said, 'And when the righteous are praised, the
peoples rejoice'.[β] So come now, and let us enter upon

a   Pr 10:7
β   Pr 29:2

the eulogy, leaving our words to be governed by God and him whose commemoration we are celebrating today. For by the prayers of that blessed [saint] we believe the door of discourse will be opened for us. Nothing that I can say is a worthy measure of his labors and his prodigious struggles; [my discourse], rather, is conformed to our limitations and the measure of our weakness, and is in accordance with the way his grace inspires us, for the grace of the discourse is his [alone]. He will receive what little we say, even if it is very small, in imitation of his Lord, who received two mites from the widow and esteemed them more than the great riches brought by others,[5] as if they were worth more, because it was all she had [to give].[6]

This saint, then, O my beloved, whose feast we now celebrate today, was from Ğmoumi,[7] a village of Tihot, which was included in the eparchate of the city of Pshati. The parents who bore him were respected and very pious. The Lord [himself] satisfies us that this is a reasonable opinion by the things he said in the holy gospels, things which pertain to this subject we are now propounding [and which lead us] to think well of the parents of this blessed [saint]. This is what he says: 'Every good tree brings forth good fruit.'[a] So according to this, the honor of the parents is known from the discipline of the children, just as the good tree is known by its fruits. Because of this, then, we have confidence in saying that the parents of this blessed [saint] were very good trees since they put forth for us this good fruit.

We begin [now], therefore, to tell you the truth as we have found it in his martyrology;[8] as it is written, 'The things we have heard we have known, and our fathers have told us.'[β] This saint, then, brought forth in this way from righteous parents was nourished in the teaching and fear of

---

a   Mt 7:17
β   Ps 78:3

the Lord, and when he grew to manhood, he manifested in himself the virtues of those who bore him. Through this he received a grace of combatting spirits and he would perform a multitude of cures on those who were ill. In this way his fame became great everywhere, and as a consequence, by the election of God, he was entrusted with the altar and summoned to [exercise] the priesthood under successive bishops[9] until the blessed abba Sarapamōn,[10] after whom he received the episcopate. The holy abba Sarapamōn was a powerful[11] man, and as zealous for the Lord his God as the prophet Elijah. When he had fulfilled [his] martyrdom, this saint [Macrobius] was installed in his place to occupy the episcopal throne by the election from on high and the agreement of the peoples. For they were all attached to him because of their zeal and their love and their trust in him.

When the holy abba Macrobius had received the episcopate, he immediately drew the peoples to the beautiful flowers, which are the holy Gospels, and spoke freely with all the people with whom the Holy Spirit had entrusted him. As a chosen shepherd of the spiritual flock of Christ, he drew them to the good and waveless harbors which are the holy commandments of the Gospels.

He was accused by the impious idolaters before the magistrates who ruled over Egypt, those whom the wicked Diocletian[12] had established: Theophanes the *tabularius*[13] and Ammonius the *reparius*.[14] These [two], with a diabolic zeal and rage, came to the city of Pshati looking for the holy bishop abba Macrobius, and they were told, 'He is in the church teaching the people'. They immediately sent some of the escort,[15] who took him from the church and brought him into the presence of the wicked [magistrates], and five others from among the clerics followed him. When the wicked [magistrates] saw the grace of God upon the face of the saint, they were amazed, for he was accomplished and full of all grace, just like the patriarch Jacob. Theophanes the *tabularius* said to him, 'Are you Macrobius, whose fame has reached us? [We are told] that you hinder everyone from [participating in] the cult of the gods, and by the spells that you teach them, lead them into the cult of the Christians'. The holy bishop said to him, 'Would that even now I were able to change you, too, from the error of the idols and draw you to the living God so that he would give you eternal life!' The wicked [Theophanes] said, 'We know that the true life is from the saviour gods who give it as grace to the men who recognize their immortality; but they also bring to a bitter death the impious ones who are not thankful for their gifts. Abandon your error now and serve the truth!' The saint said, 'All those who serve the error of the lifeless idols are drowning in the dark sea of godlessness! In serving wood and stones which have no soul they have abandoned the true God and only Saviour, he who created the heaven and the earth, the sea and all that is in it.' The wicked [Theophanes] said, 'Abandon this idea, for these words will be of no use to you at all in avoiding the great tortures we will bring upon you.' The holy bishop said, 'You terrify me with tortures, but up to now you have not carried out the things with which you terrify me.' The impious [Theophanes] said, 'I do not want to teach you wisdom[16] with these tortures, but by agreeing readily [to what we say] you might save your life without [undergoing] them.' The saint said, 'If I loved my life I would do what you tell me, but now I am in haste to go to the Lord whom I love more than the whole world.'

Then the wicked [Theophanes] was filled with rage and ordered the saint to be stretched [on the rack], and he had [the executioners] beat him with flexible[17] rods, four and four by turns, until the earth was drenched with his blood. When the wicked [man] saw the flesh of the saint covered[18] with the blood, he ordered them to stop and not to beat him [any more], and said to the righteous [Macrobius], 'You have now felt the force of the tortures, O Macrobius; sacrifice, so that I can now let you go!' The saint said to him, 'Madman, from this first trial you, too, see[19] that your

tortures cannot overcome me. For my God is within [me]
helping me to achieve the victory over you and your father,
the devil, that I may share in the inheritance of his saints in
the land of the living!'

The wicked [Theophanes] was as furious as a wild beast
and he had them melt lead in an iron pot, made the saint lie
down on his back, and when [the lead] was boiling, had
them pour it down upon[20] him through a pipe. The holy
bishop and martyr of Christ said, 'Truly, through the power
of my Lord Jesus Christ, it is like cool water in my throat!'
And the crowds cried out with one voice, 'There is one God:
he of the holy bishop apa[21] Macrobius, and there is none
other but him!' So [the wicked Theophanes) had the soldiers
surround them with their war-swords and they killed a multitude of them, who were like the thief on [Christ's] right
hand to whom, through a single confession, God opened the
gate of Paradise.

The wicked Theophanes said to Ammonius, his advisor,[22]
'What shall we do with this magician?' Ammonius said to
him, 'Let us send him to Alexandria, to Armenius the
count,[23] so that he can kill him there. We cannot even have
him tortured here lest the [whole] town perish with
him!' Then he wrote to Armenius the count a letter in this
form:

> Theophanes and Ammonius write to Armenius the
> count: Greetings! We hasten now to fulfil the
> royal commands in accordance with the order of
> the sovereign rulers.[24] This wicked Macrobius,
> then, the bishop of the city of Pshati, has been
> accused before us of teaching wickedly and turn-
> ing men's hearts from the saviour gods to the cult
> of the christians. When, therefore, I brought him
> before the tribunal I questioned him with harsh
> tortures, but seeing that the [whole] town wanted
> to perish with him, I have sent him to Your
> Reverence so that you may hear him in public, and

that in accordance with the royal laws, he may
be judged by you.

Farewell in all honor, through the providence
of the gods.

The holy abba Macrobius was bound with iron chains, put
on a boat, and taken to Alexandria to Armenius the count.
When they arrived at the city they gave the letter to the
count, and since it was already evening, he ordered [them]
to take him to the prison until the next day.

When the saint was in the prison that night, keeping watch
and making great prayers to God for the whole world, the
Lord Jesus Christ appeared to him in unspeakable glory and
said to him, 'Greetings, my elect Macrobius, good shepherd
of the spiritual flock! Take comfort and be strong! Do not
be afraid, for truly, I am with you to save you from all your
afflictions. It is only a little while before you receive the
crown of immortality and rest with all the saints.' When the
Saviour had said these things, he gave [the saint] his peace,
and in this way went up from him in great glory. And when
he had seen the Lord, the holy abba Macrobius was in great
joy in the prison.

In the morning the prison warden[25] arose to inspect the
jail, and when he saw the grace on the face of the holy apa
Macrobius he venerated him and asked him to pray for his
daughter,[26] for she was prostrated [with sickness] and like
to die. And when the saint prayed to the Lord for the young
girl, she was cured of the sickness immediately. The father of
the young girl was in great amazement at what had occurred
[so] suddenly through the prayers of this saint, and he and
all his household believed in the Lord. Again, in the same
way, crowds of others in whom were demons were cured by
a single word of his mouth in the sign of the holy cross of our
Lord Jesus Christ. He made the deaf hear, he made the lame
walk, he made the blind see,[a] and everyone was

---

a Mt 11:5, Lk 7:22

astonished at the grace of the Lord which was with the saint.
Through him a multitude believed in the Lord Jesus Christ
and received baptism, marvelling at the wonders he was doing
for those with all manners of sickness.

But when the enemies of the faith also saw all the things
which the holy abba Macrobius was doing, Satan filled their
heart with envy of the saint. They went to the count Armenius and said to him, 'How long will you trust this wicked
christian, Macrobius, who is casting multitudes of spells in
the prison? In a little while he will draw everyone from the
cult of the gods to the cult of the christians!' Straightaway
[Armenius] commanded him to be brought to him, and when
they brought him before the tribunal Armenius the count
ordered a governor, whose name was Gallianus,[27] to hear
[the holy Macrobius] in public. So when the governor had
taken his seat [on the tribunal] in a place beside the sea
which was called Posidōn,[28] he ordered them to bring to him
the holy bishop abba Macrobius. And when they brought
him to him, he said to him, 'Are you Macrobius the magician
who, we are told, casts multitudes of spells in the prison,
turning men's hearts from the gods of the kings? Sacrifice
now to the gods! Your spells will be of no avail to you, so do
not destroy your own old-age!' The saint said, 'I sacrifice to
my king in heaven, Jesus Christ my Lord, to whom I am in
haste to go. Do to me now what you will, for I have God to
help me, and he has the power to deliver me from all
your tortures.' The governor said, 'Indeed? Let us see if he
can deliver you from my hands!'[β]

Then he made the saint lie down on his back and had them
slice the whole of his body with swords. They tore the nails
out of his hands and his feet, and he had them bring vinegar,
ashes, and salt and pour them over his wounds. After this he
made them tie him to the stake and torture him with iron
scrapers[29] until the bones of his ribs[30] appeared. The saint

---

a Cf. Dan 3:15

was in great anguish through the sufferings inflicted upon
him and he raised his eyes to heaven and said, 'My Lord
Jesus Christ, you are the father of those who are oppressed
and the hope of those who have no hope: arise and help us,
for it is for your sake that we are killed every day.[a] Look
upon your servant and save the son of your maidservant,[β]
for you alone are the Lord in whom I hope'. While he was
praying, the great archangel Michael appeared to him, broke
his bonds, and at that very moment healed the pains of his
body. Straightaway he stood before the governor with no
injury[31] upon him.

Then the wicked [Gallianus] was filled with rage and said,
'By the gods! I will give you great tortures!' And at once the
wicked [man] ordered them to bring fat, oil, and pitch, pour
them into a cauldron and light a fire under them. After these
things, he had them throw the holy martyr of Christ into the
boiling cauldron. But he prayed like this, saying, 'God, who,
from the beginning, has been with his elect martyrs and has
saved them from the fire and the threat of the tortures, be
with me, too, my Lord and my God, until I put to shame
this wicked [man], and may your holy name be glorified
and blessed before all this multitude who watch my struggle
today, so that all of them might know that no other god but
you, Lord Jesus Christ my God, has power to save'. While
the God-bearing bishop was praying, the cauldron immediately stopped boiling, and at that moment, through the
power of God which was with him, he sprang up from the
cauldron, safe and sound, with no injury upon him.

The governor was amazed and disturbed [by this miracle],
and even more by the cries which the crowds shouted in his
presence, exalting God on account of the wonders which had
occurred through the noble martyr, the holy abba Macrobius.
Filled with great confusion,[32] the governor said to the saint,

---

a   Rom 8:36

β   Ps 86:16

'By the gods, O Macrobius, I will give you to the wild beasts
if you do not repent!' The saint said, 'Repentance is a good
thing, O governor, but true repentance [lies] with those who
turn from evil to good. But as for those who turn from good
to evil, the scripture says this of them: "Woe to them!"[a]'

The governor was filled with rage and incensed with the
saint, and he ordered [them] to give him to the wild beasts:
a lion, a bear,[33] a leopard, a panther, and a tiger, 'so that
(said he) there will be nothing left of his body.'[34] When they
loosed the beasts upon him, they ran at him certainly, but
when they reached him, they venerated him, [prostrating
themselves] on the ground and licking his holy feet. Oh!
how the crowds cried out at that moment, glorifying God
and saying, 'There is only the God of the holy apa Macrobius, and there is none other but him!' When the saint saw
that the grace of God was with him, [then], bound and in
the midst of the wild beasts, he gave thanks to God[35] in these
words: 'God, who so loved us that you have graced us with
the dignity of Adam before he had transgressed the law of
your commandments, when every species of animal was subject [to him] and bowed its head to him because you had
adorned him by [creating him] in your image; I thank you,
Lord, that you have made my unworthiness worthy of your
glory and your honor, and have changed for me the ferocity
of the wild beasts into gentleness. They have left me [safe]
before them, as if [they were] a ewe-lamb feeding, because
of the hope we have in your holy name. To you be the glory,
together with the Father who begot you and the Holy Spirit,
the giver of life, consubstantial with you, unto the ages
of ages. Amen.'

When the governor saw that the wild beasts did not eat
him, he commanded that they be taken away from him, and
he called the saint and said to him, 'I beseech you, teach
me, too, to make magic like you. By the gods! You will be

---

a Is 5:20

my companion and counsellor all my days!' The saint said to him, 'What companionship is there between the light and the darkness?[a] Or what agreement between Christ and Belial? I myself am no magician, and [God forbid] that I should ever practise magic. Nor should this name of "magician" be associated with any christian. It is those who serve idols who have discovered every [kind of] magic.' The governor said to him, 'The laws command that those who are ignorant and who do not accept the gifts which are wished upon them be punished for their ingratitude. Sacrifice to the gods of the king so that I can let you go!' The saint said, '[God forbid] that I should ever abandon my blessed Lord in order to worship wood and stones, for by these things both you and they will be cast into the pit of the eternal fire!'

Then the governor ordered them to tie heavy stones round his neck, put him in a boat, take him away, and throw him into the sea.[36] This command was quickly executed: the servants seized him, bound him by tying his feet to his neck, put him in a boat, took him a distance of about twelve miles[37] out to sea, and in this way cast him into the depths of the sea. But God, who looks upon the love of his elect and saves those who hope in him, ordered an angel [to save the holy Macrobius]. He lifted up the saint and set him down on dry [land] in the presence of the governor before the boat came to shore. Oh! what an effect this had on the crowds at that moment! They were all crying out with one voice, saying, 'There is only the God of the holy abba Macrobius, and there is none other but him!'

The governor was confounded[38] and filled with great rage, and said, 'By the gods, I will burn you in a fire, and [then] let us see which god can deliver you from my hands!' The saint said to him, 'In the Lord my God I put my trust; I shall not be afraid of what the pagans may do to me. I have God to help me, and he has the power to deliver me from the

a 2 Cor 6:14

fire in which you say you will burn me. Nevertheless, do what you have said, and then you will know the power of my God!' Then the wicked [governor] was filled with rage when he heard these things, and he had them bind the holy abba Macrobius, throw him into a furnace, seal it up, and heat it to excess.

When it was evening [the governor] retired and went to dinner, but the Lord remembered his servant abba Macrobius in the midst of the fire and sent his angel, just as he had done when the three holy young men were in [the furnace in] Babylon.[a] [The angel] parted the flame inside the furnace and made the inside of the furnace like a breath of cool dew, and it did the saint no harm at all. He was walking in the midst of the fire, praising God and blessing the Lord in great joy, saying, 'I thank you, Lord, that you have made me worthy to be numbered with your three holy young men and have sent your angel to me to console me. You have changed the fire for me into a breath of cool dew and have again comforted me gladly. For these things, Lord, I will praise you all my life and sing psalms to you [so long] as I live, for you have made me rejoice, my God Jesus Christ, for the good things which you have done for me. The appearance of your holy angel to me has taken away all my anguish and has given healing to my flesh. To you be the glory unto the ages of ages. Amen.'

When the night had passed and the sun had risen, the governor came proudly to the furnace, for he thought in his heart that the noble [martyr] was burnt. But by the power of Christ, the angel lifted the saint out of the furnace of fire and set him before the governor. The holy abba Macrobius answered and said to the governor, 'Did I not tell you from the start that you cannot fight against the power of God which is with his saints? Nor can the servants of Christ be destroyed by punishments of this sort.'[39]

------

a Dan 3:15-28 and 3:52-90

Then the wicked [governor], ashamed that he had been defeated by the power of God which was with the holy abba Macrobius, gave his judgment: that they take off his head. The saint rejoiced on hearing his final judgment, and when the soldiers had bound him, they took him away to take off his holy head.

They came to a house which was being built in the suburbs[40] and which belonged to the city auditor.[41] His name was Dionysius and he had a son whose name was Eusebius. The latter was standing by the workmen urging them on when he fell off the building to the ground and died instantly. When they told his father, saying, 'Your son Eusebius is dead', he came quickly to the place where he lay dead and rent his garments, tearing out the hair[42] of his head and his beard and even wanting to kill himself, for [Eusebius] was his only son. [At that moment] the soldiers passed by with the holy bishop abba Macrobius, whom they had bound and were taking [away] to put to death, and when [the saint] saw [Dionysius] in such great grief he had pity on him and said to him, 'My son, why will you kill yourself? Believe in the Lord Jesus Christ and your son will live!' But he threw himself at the feet of the saint and said, 'I beseech you, man of God, pray to the Christ–God, for whose holy name you are undergoing these sufferings, so that he will give life to my son again, and I, with him and all my house, will believe in him for ever.'

When the soldiers, as Dionysius had requested them, had given the saint a little relief from the fetters with which they had bound him, the blessed [Macrobius] threw himself on his knees and prayed, saying, 'I beseech you, my Lord Jesus Christ, Son of the living God, who raised Lazarus from among the dead on the fourth day of his [entombment],[a] who raised the son of the widow of Nain,[β] who raised the

a   Jn 11:43-44
β   Lk 7:11-15

daughter of the ruler of the synagogue,[a] who will raise
everyone on the Last Day, raise [also] this young man so
that all may know that it is you who have the power of
death and life, to the glory of your holy name, together with
your good Father and the Holy Spirit, the giver of life,
consubstantial with you, unto the ages of ages. Amen.' When
he had said these things, he breathed on the young man's
face three times, as the symbol of the holy Trinity, and signed
his forehead and his breast with the saving sign of the precious
cross. He took his right hand and cried in a great voice,
'Eusebius, son of Dionysius, my Lord Jesus Christ commands
you to rise!' And at once he immediately arose, with no
injury upon him.

Oh! how great was the shout from the crowds at that
moment, when they saw this great and incredible wonder
which came about through this saint! They were crying out
with one voice, saying, 'Great is the god of the christians, the
god of abba Macrobius, the holy bishop!' And behold! eighty
men from the crowd went to the governor crying out, saying,
'We confess that we are Christians![43] We believe in the god
of abba Macrobius!' Then [the governor] was in great anger
and wrath against these saints, and commanded a crowd of
soldiers to take them and kill them with all the [most]
wicked forms of execution, and throw their bodies into the
sea. The impious soldiers at once did as the governor had
commanded. Behold! a multitude of angels came down from
heaven with shining crowns in their hands. They greeted the
souls of the holy martyrs, placed the shining crowns upon
their heads, and joyfully took them up to him they loved,
our Lord Jesus Christ.

Then the soldiers who were in charge of the holy bishop
abba Macrobius hurried after him with all speed to take off
his head in accordance with the order of the wicked governor, and they bound him once more and walked with him to

---

a Mk 5:22-42, Lk 8:41-55

take him to the place where they would kill him. When they came to the place where he would consummate the struggle of his martyrdom, the holy bishop of Christ asked the soldiers, saying, 'If[44] it is agreeable to you, let me pray to my god before I consummate my struggle.' They said to him, 'Do what you want, our father, but hurry! We are only subordinates, and set under authority.' [Then] he turned his face to the east and prayed to the Lord, speaking like this: 'I thank you, Lord, God of my fathers, that this day and this hour you have made me worthy to be a companion in the sufferings of your Christ. Now, Lord, God of the saints, direct my way to you in peace, and do not let [the demons] who are in the air impede me. Let your angel of peace accompany me until I pass without danger the powers of darkness which are there. Remember, too, Lord, your universal church in every place: make this tempest pass which opposes it, and let this persecution which is upon your flock, scattering it everywhere, quickly cease. For it is you who care for your people and to you belongs all glory and all honor, together with your good Father and the Holy Spirit, unto the ages of ages. Amen.'

When he had said the 'Amen', he stretched out his holy neck in silence. They immediately took off his head, and in this way he gave his spirit into the hands of the Lord, with whom [he was] at that moment, the second day of the month Phamenōth.[45] His holy body remained lying [there] that day, for the soldiers were guarding it to prevent anyone from taking it [away].[46] But when it was night, the brothers of the saint came and shrouded[47] his holy body, for they had been following him since [he left] his village and had been hidden in the city of Alexandria. They put him on a boat and took him south to Ǧmoumi,[48] his village, and with them was Eucharistus, the son of Julius of Chbehs.[49] They built an illustrious sanctuary for him and laid his body in it. Oh, what a multitude of signs and wonders and

multitudinous cures occurred in his illustrious oratory[50]
through his blessed relics, and all were amazed and
were glorifying our Lord and our God and our
Saviour, Jesus Christ, through whom and
to whom belong the glory and the
honor, together with his good
Father and the Holy Spirit,
unto the ages of all ages.
Amen.[51]

NOTES

(For a List of Abbreviations the reader is referred to pages v-vi.)

1. For Pshati/Nikiou/Niqyūs/Prosōpitēs, see A, nn. 99-100.

2. I.e. 26 February (Julian)/11 March (Gregorian). See *SE*, 185; *SAJ* (832)-(835).

3. For the manuscript and edition of this work, see A, n. 111.

4. In some texts and versions of the Coptic/Arabic *Synaxarium*, Macrobius appears as Macarius (cf. also Amélineau's error noted in C, n. 26), but there is no doubt that this is a misreading. Makrobi/ Macrobius is also mentioned elsewhere: e.g. in the *Martyrdom of St Macarius of Antioch* (see C, n. 27), and the *Martyrdom of Apa Ari*: 'For in these days the martyrdom of the truly thrice-blessed and honorable abba Makrobi, the most pious bishop of this diocese (for *thōš* [Bo] as 'diocese', see the *Life of Shenoute*, 94, n. 8) of Pshati, also took place in Alexandria' (Hyvernat, *Actes*, 214).

5. Following the emendation suggested by Hyvernat in *ibid.*, 226, n. 2.

6. As Hyvernat observes *(ibid.,* 226, n. 1), there is an obvious similarity—sometimes an identity—between this prologue to the *Martyrdom of Saint Macrobius* and that of the *Martyrdom of Saint Peter of Alexandria*. From the observations we made earlier—see especially C, n. 21—this should cause us no surprise.

7. For Ğmoumi/Ğmouni/Ashmūn (the *Synaxarium* reads Ashmūn Kharīsāt [*SAJ* (832)]), see C, n. 26.

8. *Martyrologion* (Gr: see Lampe, *Lexicon,* 830). The oldest extant martyrology is the Syriac Calendar of Antioch which was compiled, originally in Greek, between 362 and 381. The greek text is now lost, but we have a syriac summary dating from the early fifth century. In seventh-century Egypt there were certainly local martyrologies in circulation, but according to KHS-Burmester, the first recension of the Arabic *Synaxarium* in use today dates only from the late twelfth or early thirteenth century. It was almost certainly compiled by Peter Severus al-Gamīl, bishop of Malīg, and this recension seems then to have been used as a basis for the longer and better-known version of Michael, bishop of Athrīb and Malīg, writing perhaps half a century later. It is Michael's compilation which, with some additions, is used in the Coptic church today. See O. H. E. KHS-Burmester, 'On the Date and Authorship of the Arabic Synaxarium of the Coptic Church', *Journal of*

Theological Studies 39 (1938) 249-253; G. Graf, 'Zur Autorschaft des arabischen Synaxars der Kopten', *Orientalia* N.S. 9 (1940) 240-243; *GCAL* 2: 340-344, 416-427.

9. Lit. 'under the bishops according to the time'.

10. Sarapamōn is fairly well documented. He was born in Jerusalem of a jewish family and originally named Simeon, but after his parents' death he decided to convert to Christianity. John, the bishop of Jerusalem, agreed to give him instruction, but not to baptize him since he was afraid of provoking the Jews. He therefore sent him to Theonas, the sixteenth coptic patriarch, in Alexandria, and it was Theonas who initiated him into Christianity. Sarapamōn then entered the monastic life at the monastery of the Ennaton (see Timm, *Das christlich-koptischen Ägypten* 2: 833-853), and after Theonas' death assisted his successor Peter I in the administration of the patriarchate. Shortly afterwards he was ordained bishop of Nikiou. During the Great Persecution, Diocletian summoned him to Antioch and, after interrogation, sent him back to Alexandria where he was imprisoned and tortured. The governor of Alexandria then gave him into the charge of Satrius Arrianus, the provincial governor of the Thebaid and one of the most savage of the persecutors (see Reymond/Barns, *Four Martyrdoms,* 7, n. 23), who happened to be visiting Alexandria at the time. Arrianus therefore took Sarapamōn with him on his return journey up the Nile, but when the boat reached Nikiou it would move no further. Arrianus then had Sarapamōn taken ashore and beheaded. He is commemorated in the *Synaxarium* on 28 Hathōr = 7 December in the Gregorian calendar. See *SE,* 244-245; *SAJ* (273)-(277); Hyvernat, *Actes,* 304-331 (an epic martyrdom, incomplete at the beginning and with a few lacunae).

11. *Dynatos* (Gr). The meaning here is 'powerful' in the sense of virtuous, charismatic, strong in the faith, with strength of soul (cf. Lampe, *Lexicon,* 392).

12. See the Introduction to the *Martyrdom of Macrobius,* pp. 101-102.

13. For Theophanes/Diophanes the *tabularius* (an official whose main duties lay in the assessment and collection of the land-tax: see G. Rouillard, *L'administration civile de l'Égypte byzantine* [Paris, 1928²] 92), see C, n. 27.

14. Ammonius appears in A. H. M. Jones, J. R. Martindale, and J. Morris, *The Prosopography of the Later Roman Empire I* (Cambridge, 1971) 55, where he is referred to as an official in the Thebaid *c.* 298 who possessed police functions. More precisely, a *reparius/riparius* was a sort of local chief of police who was primarily responsible for the maintenance of public order. It was also his duty

to ensure that arrested malefactors were kept safely in custody and appeared before the court at the proper time. See further Rouillard, *L'administration civile,* 156, 163-166.

15.   *Taxis* (Gr): the body of troops who were accompanying them.

16.   Lit. 'I do not want you to become wise'.

17.   Lit. 'fresh, soft, pliable'. This beating, the number of executioners, the earth drenched with blood, and so on, are all standard *topoi* in the epic martyrdoms.

18.   Lit. 'being under the blood'.

19.   Lit. 'think'.

20.   This is what the text reads, but from what Macrobius says in the next sentence it is clear that the lead is being poured down his throat. The torture, the accompanying miracle, Macrobius's reply, the conversion of the onlookers and their subsequent martyrdom, are all standard material.

21.   On the titles *apa* and *abba,* which interchange in this martyrdom, see the *Life of Shenoute,* 93, n. 2.

22.   *Synkathedros* (Gr): the term means literally 'someone sitting beside you'. I.e. an assessor, assistant, adviser. See Mason, *Greek Terms,* 88; Lampe, *Lexicon,* 1267.

23.   Armenius, the *komēs* (Gr)/*comes* (Lat) of Alexandria, is well known in the martyrdoms, and only Arrianus is cited more frequently. Armenius was *comes* from 303 to at least 307, and the best account of him and his titles is to be found in Vandersleyen, *Chronologie des préfets* (see B, n. 7) 92. There is a shorter account in Jones, Martindale, and Morris, *Prosopography* 1:108.

24.   *Autokratōr* (Gr): the reference is to Diocletian and Galerius.

25.   A *komentarēsios* (Gr)/*commentariensis* (Lat) (see Mason, *Greek Terms,* 62; Rouillard, *L'administration civile,* 151, 162) was an official who, among other related duties, kept a list of the prisoners in a jail, and was a sort of combination of court-recorder and assistant to the prison-governor (I have called him the 'prison warden', but there is no precise english equivalent). In this case the *commentariensis* is undoubtedly Julius of Chbehs/Aqfahs (see *SAJ* [833] and n. 49 below), and the mention of his name therefore assigns the martyrdoms of Macrobius to the so-called Julius of Aqfahs Cycle of martyrdoms (see Delehaye, *Martyrs d'Egypte,* 138: he appears in the passions of a dozen other martyrs). According to the *Synaxarium* he was a crypto-Christian in the employ of the pagan authorities, but God protected him by ensuring that they never noticed this. Julius was therefore in a position in which he could talk to the martyrs, encourage them, record their stories, and, when their passions had been fulfilled, collect

their relics for proper veneration. Towards the end of the Great Persecution, he too became inflamed with the desire to follow in their
footsteps and went to Arfānyūs, governor of Sammanūd, to profess
himself a Christian. He was interrogated, tortured, required to recant,
and then, having refused, was sent to the governor of Atrīb who inflicted upon him further tortures. 'But our Lord the Messiah preserved
him from all harm: three times he died and three times he was
resurrected by him' (*SAJ* [291]). He then went to Alexander, governor
of Ṭawah, who was so reluctant to condemn him that Julius had to
force him to do so (at his command his servants drew their swords and
said to Alexander, 'If you do not condemn us, we will kill you').
Eventually, therefore, he was executed, and with him died his son,
his brother, his servants, and some fifteen hundred other persons,
including the governors of Sammanūd and Atrīb, all of whom had been
converted by the heroic sufferings of the saint (see *SAJ* [76]-[78];
SE, 174-175 [which is not quite accurate]). Julius fills an important
role in the epic martyrdoms, for if there were no-one 'on the inside',
how could one know all the details—sometimes confidential—of what
had transpired?

26.   Her name was Eucharistia, but the account in the *Synaxarium*
transforms Julius's daughter Eucharistia into his son Eucharistos, and
adds that he was paralyzed in his hands and his feet (see *SAJ*
[833]; *SE,* 185). See also n. 49 below.

27.   I have been able to find no further information on Kellianos/
Gallianus, and it is most unlikely, in the circumstances, that the name
is a distortion of the well-known Koukianos/Culcianus (see Vandersleyen, *Chronologie des préfets,* 87-90, 93; Jones, Martindale, and
Morris, *Prosopography* 1:233-234).

28.   Posidōn is Poseidion, the promontory, partly natural and partly
artificial, which extended into the harbor at Alexandria. There was
a temple to Poseidon built upon it and also a palace, the Timoneion,
in which, presumably, Gallianus held the tribunal. So far as I know,
no trace now remains of this structure. See P. M. Fraser, *Ptolemaic
Alexandria* (Oxford, 1972) 1:22-24, 2:66-67, n. 153.

29.   Hyvernat renders *hoks* (Bo) by 'iron hooks (?)' (*Actes,* 235), but
there is no doubt that the instruments are scrapers (see Crum,
Dictionary, 663a). They appear in a number of martyrdoms.

30.   *Kasbēt* (Bo): see *ibid.* 119b.

31.   Lit. 'destruction'.

32.   *Šphit* (Bo): the basic meaning is 'shame' (see *ibid.* 577a), but we
can also translate it by such terms as embarrassment or confusion.

33.   *Laboi* (Bo): both the Coptic word and its Ancient Egyptian

prototype can mean a bear or a lioness, but here, for the sake of variety, it is surely the former.

34.   I.e. so that there would be no relics left to act as the focus for yet another martyr-cult. As early as the martyrdom of Polycarp in the middle of the second century his bones were described as 'more valuable than jewels and finer than gold' (Musurillo, *Acts of the Christian Martyrs*, 16-17), and there is no doubt that this reflects an idea which had already been in existence for a considerable period. By the time of the Great Persecution, relics were of first importance in popular Christianity. See also pages 99-101 above, and nn. 39, 46, and 50 below.

35.   *Exomologia* (Bo)/*Exomologeomai* (Gr) may also mean 'confessed' or 'bore witness' (see Lampe, *Lexicon*, 499).

36.   Lit. 'into the sea (*pelagos* [Gr]) of the sea (*iom* [Bo])'. I.e. into the open sea, the depths of the sea.

37.   The Greco-Roman mile was about 1480 meters, but this is simply a standard *topos* in the martyrdoms.

38.   Or shamed, or perplexed, or embarrassed: see n. 32 above.

39.   Cf. Reymond/Barns, *Four Martyrdoms*, 17: 'The hero of a martyrology of any length will certainly find himself shut in a furnace at least once; but since Ananias, Azarias and Misael emerged from the furnace unscathed, so should he; anything an Old Testament character can do a Christian martyr can do as well, or better. Decapitation, however, is a treatment from which S. John the Baptist himself failed to recover'. There is also the problem of relics: a successful incineration would destroy all vestiges of the martyr, and as we observed above in n. 34, relics were too valuable for that. The episode of the governor taking time off from these brutalities to go and have dinner is also a regular occurrence (see Delehaye, *Martyrs d'Égypte*, 146).

40.   For *proastion* (Bo)/*proasteion* (Gr) as a suburban house, see Lampe, *Lexicon*, 1138.

41.   The *logistēs* (Bo/Gr) of the city was the *curator civitatis* (Lat), an official who controlled the finances of the city, but who, as a consequence of this, had considerable power and influence in most other areas of local government. See B. R. Rees, 'The *Curator Civitatis* in Egypt', *Journal of Juristic Papyrology* 7 (1953-54) 83-105; the *Oxford Classical Dictionary*, 301 *s.v. Curator Rei Publicae*; Mason, *Greek Terms*, 66 *s.v. logistēs*; Rouillard, *L'administration civile*, 66.

42.   *Phōi* (Bo) is simply an alternative spelling for *foi* 'hair'.

43.   Lit. 'We are Christians, openly/confessedly'. The words, the incident, and the ensuing martyrdom of these new converts are all standard material.

44.   Reading *isje* for *isjen*.

45. See n. 2 above.
46. So that there would be no relics: see n. 34 above.
47. Lit. 'wrapped, swathed'.
48. See n. 7 above.
49. See nn. 25-26 above.
50. *Euktērion* (Bo/Gr): see Lampe, *Lexicon*, 566 *s.v. euktērios* § B. The practice of building a sanctuary or oratory over a martyr's relics seems to have begun with Constantine. These *martyria* normally had no fixed altars and were used for intercession, not for regular worship. There would be an annual festival at the site on the martyr's birthday, and it is clear from Shenoute's strictures that these events could quite frequently get out of hand (see the material cited in C, n. 5 above). Further on the *martyria,* see the article in the *New Catholic Encyclopaedia* (New York, 1967) 9:316-317 (with bibliography).
51. The account in the *Synaxarium* of these final events in the life of Macrobius is rather different. The brothers of the saint, Jonas and Isaac, together with Mary, his sister, come to visit him in prison, but then, after he has comforted them, they return home. It is then Julius of Aqfaḥs who shrouds Macrobius's body, places a cross on his breast, and sends the remains to Nikiou with his servants. But when the boat moored at Ğmoumi/Ashmūn, it would go no further (a common *topos*), and a voice came from the corpse saying that it was there, in Ashmūn, that God wished the body to remain. The *Synaxarium* adds that Macrobius lived for 131 years, of which eight were spent as a deacon, thirty as a priest, and thirty-nine as bishop of Nikiou (see *SAJ* [834]).

SELECT
BIBLIOGRAPHY

SELECT BIBLIOGRAPHY

A) EGYPTIAN CHRISTIANITY AND EARLY ISLĀM

For the study of Coptic–Muslim relations in the period immediately before, during, and after the Arab invasion, certain texts are either useful or essential. First of all, reference must be made to the following works which contain vital bibliographical information:

Butler, A. J., ed. by P. M. Fraser, *The Arab Conquest of Egypt*, Oxford, 1978 (second edition), pages v-xi, xlv-lxxxiii.
Orlandi, T., *Elementi di Lingua e Letteratura Copta*, Milan, 1970, pages 59-158.
———, 'The Future of Studies in Coptic Biblical and Ecclesiastical Literature', in R. McL. Wilson, ed., *The Future of Coptic Studies*, Leiden, 1978, 143-163.
———, 'Coptic Literature', in B. E. Pearson and J. E. Goehring, eds., *The Roots of Egyptian Christianity*, Philadelphia, 1986, 51-81.

The christian arab writers of the period are dealt with in the first two volumes of Georg Graf's magisterial *Geschichte der Christlichen Arabischen Literatur*, Studi e Testi 118. Vatican City, 1944-1953, supplemented by Khalil Samir, 'Arabic Sources for Early Egyptian Christianity', in Pearson and Goehring, *Roots of Egyptian Christianity*, 82-97.

Secondly, by far the most accurate and readable introduction to egyptian Christianity is to be found in Aziz S. Atiya, *History of Eastern Christianity*, London, 1967: Notre Dame, 1968, Part I: pages 1-145. Atiya also provides a considerable amount of further bibliographical material.

Thirdly, the following volumes all contain useful information:

Abū Ṣāliḥ, ed./tr. by B. T. A. Evetts, *The Churches and Monasteries of Egypt and Some Neighbouring Countries Attributed to Abū Ṣāliḥ, the Armenian*, Oxford, 1895. In Arabic and English.
Alcock, A., ed./tr., *The Life of Samuel of Kalamun by Isaac the Presbyter*. Warminster, 1983 (cf. Butler/Fraser, *Arab Conquest of Egypt*,

xlix [ii]). In Coptic and English
Amélineau, E., *La géographie de l'Égypte à l'époque copte*. Paris, 1893;
     rpt. Osnabrück 1973. Despite its age, this remains an indispensable
     reference work, but it must now be supplemented by the studies of
     Bey, Calderini, Munier, and (especially) Timm, *q.v.*
Bey, M. Ramzi, 'Rectifications à l'ouvrage d'É. Amélineau, *Géographie
     de l'Égypte à l'époque copte*', in *Mélanges Maspero: III, Orient
     Islamique*, Mémoires publiés par les membres de l'Institut français
     d'archéologie orientale du Caire, Tome 68, Cairo, 1940, 273-321.
     This article, unfortunately for Westerners, is entirely in Arabic.
Butler, A. J., ed. P. M. Fraser, *The Arab Conquest of Egypt*. Oxford,
     1902; 1978 (second edition). The second edition includes:
     Idem, The Treaty of Miṣr in Ṭabarī, Oxford, 1902; and
     Idem, Babylon of Egypt: A Study in the History of Old Cairo.
     Oxford, 1914. Butler's beautifully written work remains in-
     dispensable.
Calderini, A., *Dizionario dei Nomi Geografici e Topografici dell'Egitto
     Greco-Romano*. Cairo/Milan, 1935–. At the time of writing (1987)
     this encyclopaedic compilation has reached the letter *sigma*.
Cauwenbergh, P. van, *Étude sur les moines d'Égypte depuis le concile
     de Chalcédoine (451) jusqu'à l'invasion arabe (640)*. Paris, 1914;
     rpt. Milan 1973.
Charles, R. H., *The Chronicle of John, Coptic Bishop of Nikiou*, Text
     and Translation Society 3. London, 1916; rpt. Amsterdam n.d.
     English only; for the Ethiopic text, see *s.v.* Zotenberg, H.
Coquin, R.-G., ed./tr., *Livre de la consécration du sanctuaire de
     Benjamin*, Bibliothèque d'études coptes, Tome 13. Cairo, 1975.
     A superb edition in Coptic, Arabic, and French.
Lane–Poole, S., *A History of Egypt in the Middle Ages*. London, 1936
     (fifth edition). An old standard history.
Malan, S. C., *A Short History of the Copts and of Their Church
     Translated from the Arabic of Tāqi-ed-Dīn El-Maqrīzī*. London,
     1873. This is a translation of the first four chapters of Maqrīzī's
     text and ends at page 81 of Wüstenfeld's german version (*q.v.*).
Meinardus, O., *Christian Egypt: Ancient and Modern*. Cairo, 1977[2].
Michael of Athrīb and Malīg, ed./tr. by R. Basset, *Le Synaxaire Arabe
     Jacobite (Rédaction Copte)*. This is to be found in six separate
     sections in six different volumes of the *Patrologia Orientalis*. For
     details of the pagination, which is somewhat complicated, see the
     List of Abbreviations on page v above *s.v.* SAJ. Much of the
     material may be found in English in E. A. Wallis Budge, *The Book
     of the Saints of the Ethiopian Church* (Cambridge 1928; rpt.

Hildesheim 1976 [four volumes in two]), since the Ethiopic *Synaxarium* was based directly on that of Michael of Athrīb.

Müller, C. D. G., 'Benjamin I, 38. Patriarch von Alexandrien', *Le Muséon* 69 (1956) 313-340.

————, 'Neues über Benjamin I, 38. und Agathon, 39., Patriarchen von Alexandrien', *Le Muséon* 72 (1959) 323-347.

Munier, H., 'La géographie de l'Égypte d'après les listes copto-arabes', *Bulletin de la Société d'Archéologie Copte* 5 (1939) 201-243.

O'Leary, De L., *The Saints of Egypt.* New York 1937; rpt. Amsterdam 1974.

Severus/Sāwirūs ibn al-Muqaffaʿ, ed./tr. by B. T. A. Evetts, *History of the Patriarchs of the Coptic Church of Alexandria.* This is to be found in four separate sections in three different volumes of the *Patrologia Orientalis.* For the pagination, see the List of Abbreviations on page v. In Arabic and English. It is a work of the first importance.

Timm, S., *Das Christlich-Koptische Ägypten in Arabischer Zeit.* Wiesbaden, 1984–. Three volumes of this invaluable and detailed gazeteer have so far appeared.

Tisserant, E. and Wiet, G., 'La liste des patriarches d'Alexandrie dans Qalqachandi', *Revue de l'Orient Chrétien* 23 (1922-23) 123-143.

Wüstenfeld, F., *Macrizi's Geschichte der Copten.* Göttingen, 1845. In Arabic and German.

Zotenberg, H., ed./tr., *Chronique de Jean, évêque de Nikiou.* Paris, 1883. In Ethiopic and French.

B) ISAAC OF ALEXANDRIA

See *ACE*, 548-552; *HP* (275)-(280); *SAJ* (191)-(192); Budge; *Book of the Saints of the Ethiopian Church*, 1:224-225.

Amélineau, E., *Histoire du patriarche copte Isaac*, Publications de l'École des Lettres d'Alger: Bulletin de correspondance Africaine II. Paris, 1890. In Coptic and French.

————, 'Sur deux documents coptes écrits sous la domination arabe', *Bulletin de l'Institut d'Égypte (Cairo)* Ser. 2 Vol. 6 (1885) 324-369.

Chaîne, M., 'La durée du patriarcat d'Isaac, XLIᵉ Patriarche d'Alexandrie', *Revue de l'Orient Chrétien* 23 (ser. 3,3) (1922-23) 214-216.

Jülicher, A., 'Die Liste der alexandrinischen Patriarchen im 6. und 7. Jahrhundert', in *Festgabe von Fachgenossen und Freunden Karl Müller*, Tübingen, 1922, 7-23.

Lee, G. M., 'Coptic Christianity in a Changing World', in S. Mews, ed., *Religion and National Identity*, Studies in Church History 48. Oxford, 1982, 39-45.

Porcher, E., *Vie d'Isaac, Patriarche d'Alexandrie de 686 à 689*, Patrologia Orientalis, Volume 9 Fascicle 3. Paris, 1914; rpt. Turnhout 1974. In Coptic and French.

———, 'Les dates du patriarcat d'Isaac', *Revue de l'Orient Chrétien* 24 (ser. 3,4) (1924) 219-222.

Rizzitano, U., ' 'Abd al-'Azīz B. Marwān, Governatore Umayyade d'Egitto', *Atti della Reale Accademia dei Lincei, Rendiconti* Series 8,2 (1941) 321-347.

C) COPTIC MARTYRDOMS

Firstly, an essential bibliography is provided in:
E. A. E. Reymond and J. W. B. Barns, eds./trs., *Four Martyrdoms From the Pierpont Morgan Coptic Codices*. Oxford, 1973, pages ix-xii.

Secondly, for the background to the martyrdoms, see:
Frend, W. H. C., *Martyrdom and Persecution in the Early Church*. Oxford, 1965. This is the standard study on the subject.
Workman, H. B., *Persecution in the Early Church*. Oxford, 1906; rpt. 1980. Despite its age, this still remains a valuable, brief introduction.

Thirdly, for the literary forms of the martyrdoms, see:
Delehaye, H., *Les martyrs d'Égypte*. Brussels, 1923. This study was first published in volume 40 of *Analecta Bollandiana*, and was then republished in 1923 as a separate volume.
———, *Les passions des martyrs et les genres littéraires*, Subsidia Hagiographica xiiiB. Brussels, 1966 (second edition). An essential work.

Fourthly, there are substantial collections of martyrdoms with translations into English, French, German, and Latin in the following volumes:

Balestri, I. and Hyvernat, H., *Acta Martyrum I-II*, CSCO 43 and 86 (textus); CSCO 44 and 125 (versio). Louvain, 1907-55. In Coptic and Latin.

Budge, E. A. T. Wallis, *Coptic Martyrdoms, etc. in the Dialect of Upper Egypt*, London, 1941; rpt. New York, 1977. In Coptic and English (neither Budge's editions nor his translations are always reliable).

Hyvernat, H., *Les Actes des martyrs de l'Égypte*. Paris, 1886; rpt. Hildesheim, 1977. In Coptic and French.

Reymond and Barns, *Four Martyrdoms From the Pierpont Morgan Coptic Codices*, cited above. In Coptic and English.

Till, W., *Koptische Heiligen- und Martyrerlegende*, Orientalis christiana analecta 102. Rome, 1935-36. In Coptic and German.

Fifthly and finally, for assistance in identifying the *dramatis personae* of the martyrdoms, the following volumes are invaluable:

Jones, A. H. M., Martindale, J. R., and Morris, J., *The Prosopography of the Later Roman Empire*, Volume I. Cambridge, 1971.

Lallemand, J., *L'administration civile de l'Égypte, 284-382*. Brussels, 1964.

Rouillard, G., *L'administration civile de l'Égypte byzantine*. Paris, 1928 (second edition).

Vandersleyen, C., *Chronologie des préfets d'Égypte de 284 à 395*, Collection Latomus 55. Brussels, 1962.

The above lists are not intended to be comprehensive, and a glance at Fraser's Additional Bibliography in the second edition of Butler's *Arab Conquest of Egypt*, xlv-lxxxiii, will show just how uncomprehensive they are. The works cited, however, represent those which I found most useful and which have been most frequently cited in this present study. With the exception of M. Ramzi Bey's article, I have avoided listing works entirely in Arabic, but mention must be made of the series at present being published under the directorship of Néophytos Edelby and Khalil Samir, *Patrimoine Arabe Chrétien: Textes et Études de Littérature Arabe Chrétienne Ancienne* (available from the Pontificio Istituto Orientale in Rome), of which a dozen volumes have now been printed. One might also notice M. Sayyid Kīlāni's *Al-Adab al-Qibṭi Qadīman wa-Ḥadīthan (Coptic Literature, Old and New)* (Cairo 1962), which is, so far as I know, the only attempt made so far at providing a comprehensive history of Coptic literature (it is a volume of 240 pages and contains useful bibliographical information).

INDEX OF PROPER NAMES

A) PERSONAL NAMES

B = Bishop   E = Emperor   M = Monk
C = Caliph   G = Governor   P = Patriarch

*An asterisk * indicates that the word is accompanied by an explanatory note.*

143

B)   GEOGRAPHICAL
     NAMES

INDEX OF WORDS AND TECHNICAL TERMS
IN ARABIC, COPTIC, ETHIOPIC, GREEK, LATIN, AND SYRIAC

CISTERCIAN PUBLICATIONS INC.

Kalamazoo, Michigan

TITLES LISTING

THE CISTERCIAN FATHERS SERIES

Texts and Studies
in the
Monastic Tradition

* Temporarily out of print   *† Forthcoming*

THE CISTERCIAN STUDIES SERIES

Temporarily out of print   †*Forthcoming*

Eight Chapters on Perfection and Angel's Song
   (Walter Hilton)

Creative Suffering (Iulia de Beausobre)

Bringing Forth Christ. Five Feasts of the Child
   Jesus (St Bonaventure)

Gentleness in St John of the Cross

Distributed in North America only for Fairacres Press.

DISTRIBUTED BOOKS

St Benedict: Man with An Idea (Melbourne Studies)

The Spirit of Simplicity

Benedict's Disciples (David Hugh Farmer)

The Emperor's Monk: A Contemporary Life of
   Benedict of Aniane

A Guide to Cistercian Scholarship (2nd ed.)

*North American customers may order
through booksellers or directly
from the publisher:*

Cistercian Publications
WMU Station
Kalamazoo, Michigan 49008
(616) 383-4985

*Cistercian Publications are available in
Britain, Europe and the Common-
wealth through A. R. Mowbray &
Co Ltd   St Thomas House   Oxford
OX1 1SJ.
For a sterling price list, please consult
Mowbray's General Catalogue.*

*A complete catalogue of texts-in-
translation and studies on early,
medieval, and modern Christian
monasticism is available at no cost
from Cistercian Publications.*

*Cistercian monks and nuns have been
living lives of prayer & praise, meditation &
manual labor since the twelfth century.
They are part of an unbroken tradition
which extends back to the fourth century
and which continues today in the Catholic
church, the Orthodox churches, the
Anglican communion, and, most recently,
in the Protestant churches.*

*Share their way of life and their search for
God by reading Cistercian Publications.*

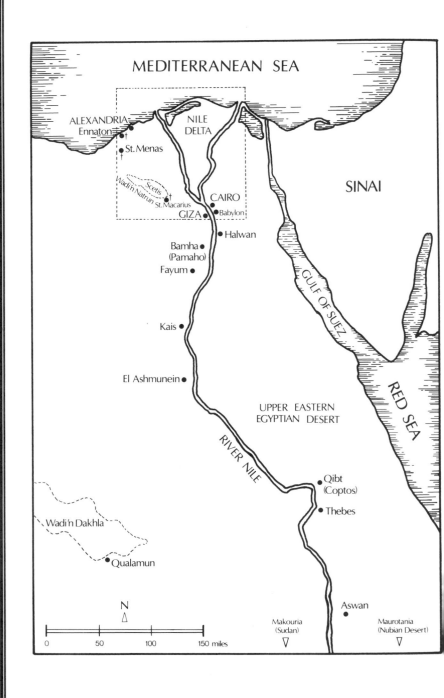